PURE SIMPLE COOKING

effortless meals every day

PURE SIMPLE
COOKING

DIANA HENRY

photography by Jonathan Lovekin

TEN SPEED PRESS
Berkeley | Toronto

to Gillies, with love

Ten Speed Press
PO Box 7123
Berkeley, CA 94707
www.tenspeed.com

First published in Great Britain in 2007 by Mitchell Beazley,
under the title *Cook Simple*
an imprint of Octopus Publishing Group Ltd
2-4 Heron Quays, Docklands, London E14 4JP

Distributed in Canada by Ten Speed Press Canada.

Commissioning Editor: Rebecca Spry
Art Director: Tim Foster
Designer: Miranda Harvey
Editors: Susan Fleming, Debbie Robertson
Proofreader: Jamie Ambrose
Home Economist: Sarah Lewis
Production Controller: Lucy Carter
Index: John Noble

Typeset in Garamond and Din
Color reproduction by Sang Choy, Singapore
Printed and bound by Toppan, China

Library of Congress Cataloging-in-Publication Data
Henry, Diana.
  Pure simple cooking : effortless meals every day / Diana
Henry ; photography by Jonathan Lovekin.
     p. cm.
  Originally published: Great Britain : Mitchell Beazley, 2007.
  Includes index.
  Summary: "An everyday cookbook with 150 recipes that
feature simple food enhanced with fresh ingredients"
—Provided by publisher.
  ISBN 978-1-58008-948-7
  1. Quick and easy cookery. I. Title.
  TX833.5.H477 2009
  641.5'55—dc22
                                    2008035099

Printed in China
First printing, 2009
1 2 3 4 5 6 7 8 9 10 — 13 12 11 10 09

contents

· · · · · ·

introduction

......

An eager cook, I used to dash around convenience stores after work trying to think of something for supper, envying those who could spend more time in their kitchens. I'm not an aficionado of the frozen dinner. Even after a tough day I prefer to spend 15 minutes cooking spaghetti and tossing it with olive oil, garlic, and red pepper flakes than the same amount of time waiting to eat the contents of an aluminum foil pan that will feed only one person when it says it will do two.

But when I had a baby, my cooking changed. "Quick" cooking was no longer the answer; I couldn't stir a risotto for 25 minutes with a baby on my hip. I needed *effortless* cooking. I had to find simple ways to turn the building blocks of meals — chicken thighs, chops, a few bell peppers — into something that would make me salivate as well as sustain me.

The first thing I did was throw nearly everything in the oven, which takes less time than you'd think. A jointed chicken cooks in 40 minutes, a small leg of lamb in 50, and fillets of fish in 12. An ever-growing range of marinades kept me roasting and baking vegetables and meat for months. When I got tired of marinating, I served roasted meat and fish with pestos, salsas, and savory butters that could be whirled in the blender. I plundered the cuisines of every country I could think of for ways to accessorize simple offerings.

Even desserts got the oven treatment. Baked fruit might sound boring, but try it doused in red wine and cassis, cooked *very* slowly and served with a big bowl of cream — better than any slaved-over bit of pastry. One-dish cooking also became vital: vegetables were stuck in with the meat, and I acquired winning ways with little potatoes, roasting them with spices, glazed with balsamic vinegar, or drizzled with pesto. Green salad became ubiquitous.

There are plenty of faster dishes in this book too. Lots of them are quite restaurant-y and ideal for last-minute supper parties. Seared tuna or chicken can be dressed up with the same sauces as roast beef. A bag of greens can be tossed with other ingredients — figs, prosciutto, and pomegranate seeds, for instance — which require only a bit of shopping.

Finding ways of cooking that involve spending no more than 15 minutes at the kitchen counter (though the meal might take longer to cook) has made me more creative: I have looked again at what I can do with a jar of tahini, a can of anchovies, or a bag of pears. It has also made me more sociable. These days I can have friends for supper midweek (even with a job and two children) and not end up frazzled.

Whether you have a punishing job, are juggling kids, or are single and just want ideas for no-hassle entertaining, if you like your food simple, this book will help you to make it better.

7

chicken
......

A recipe, from a café in Hawaii, which I have been making for years. There's practically no cooking, but everyone loves this dish — it's always hard to resist sweet, honey-glazed meat. Serve with rice and stir-fried greens, or in good weather, a salad of greens, shredded scallions, and julienned (fine strips) cucumber and carrot.

• • • • • •

pacific lime chicken

serves 4

marinade

5 tbsp honey

5 tbsp dark soy sauce

juice of 4 limes

1 tbsp light brown sugar

3 cloves garlic, crushed or grated

leaves from 5 sprigs thyme

black pepper

8 chicken thighs, bone in, skin on

wedges or halves of lime, to serve

I Mix all the marinade ingredients together. Make incisions in the underside of the chicken and pour the marinade over it. Cover with plastic wrap. If you have time, leave the chicken to marinate — from 15 minutes to the whole afternoon — in the refrigerator, turning the chicken pieces every so often.

2 Preheat the oven to 375°F. Lift the chicken out of the marinade and put it in a small roasting pan or shallow gratin dish; it needs to lie in a single layer. Roast for 35 to 40 minutes, basting every so often with the cooking juices until cooked through. If it gets too dark in color, cover the dish with aluminum foil. The finished dish will be sticky and glossy. Serve with the limes.

and also...

roast catalan chicken

Cook in the same way as above but make the marinade from ¼ cup olive oil, ½ cup honey, the juice of 1 lemon, 1 tbsp ground cumin, 6 crushed garlic cloves, salt, and pepper. Serve with little roasted potatoes and a big green salad.

Here is good old roast chicken and then some. I like it because all the veggies are served in one dish and there's no gravy to make: just prepare the sauce in advance and spoon the cooking juices over the meat.
In summer, I don't even bother to roast the tomatoes — simply toss in halved cherry tomatoes. And instead of potatoes, you could serve rinsed cannellini beans straight from the can.

· · · · · ·

roast chicken with warm vegetables and arugula cream

serves 4 to 6

extra virgin olive oil

1 (4-lb) roasting chicken

salt and pepper

12 oz cherry tomatoes

1¼ lbs small new potatoes

8 oz green beans, topped, but leave the tails intact

juice of ½ small lemon

arugula cream

½ cup mayonnaise

⅓ cup fromage blanc (or substitute crème fraîche)

3 oz (about 1 cup) arugula

1 Preheat the oven to 400ºF. Drizzle olive oil over the chicken and season it with salt and pepper. Roast for 1½ hours. The chicken is cooked when the juices that run between the leg and breast are clear, without any pink.

2 Meanwhile, put the tomatoes in a roasting pan, season with salt and pepper, and drizzle with a little olive oil. Roast with the chicken for 25 minutes.

3 With 20 minutes of roasting time left, boil the potatoes in salted water for about 15 minutes until tender, then drain. Cook the beans in boiling water for about 5 minutes to retain some crunch. Drain and rinse in cold water so that they stay green.

4 Slice the potatoes into a bowl. Add the tomatoes and beans and gently toss them with salt, pepper, 3 tbsp olive oil, and the lemon juice.

5 To make the arugula cream, combine the mayonnaise, fromage blanc, and arugula in a food processor and puree. Scrape into a bowl and refrigerate.

6 Divide the vegetables among plates and carve the chicken, or serve the chicken on a big warm platter with the vegetables spooned around it. Serve the arugula cream in a bowl or gravy boat on the side.

There are different kinds of chorizo sausage — some you have to cook, others you can either cook or eat as they are, and a few you don't cook at all. Try to get the second type for this dish. Chorizo also comes in sweet and hot forms, so use whichever you prefer.

. . . . . .

chicken and chorizo in rioja

serves 4

1 tbsp olive oil

8 chicken thighs, bone in, skin on

salt and pepper

1 celery stalk, finely chopped

1 large onion, halved and cut into thin slices

2 red bell peppers, halved, seeded, and cut into strips

12 oz chorizo sausage (papery skin removed), cut into ¼-inch rounds

1½ tbsp all-purpose flour

1 cup red Rioja or other red wine

1 cup chicken stock

3 sprigs thyme

1 bay leaf

2 tbsp chopped fresh flat-leaf parsley, to serve

I Preheat the oven to 350°F. Heat the oil over medium to high heat in a broad shallow casserole or Dutch oven in which the chicken can lie in a single layer (I use a shallow 12-inch Le Creuset pan). Season the chicken with salt and pepper and quickly brown it on both sides. You just want to color the outside, not cook it through. Remove the chicken and set aside.

2 Add the celery, onion, peppers, and chorizo to the pan in which you have cooked the chicken and, over medium heat, cook until the vegetables have softened, stirring frequently, about 10 minutes. Add the flour and stir it in over low heat for about 1½ minutes, then pour in the wine. Let this bubble away for a few minutes, then add the stock. Bring to a boil, then turn down to a simmer, and return the chicken to the pan, skin-side up. Season, going easy on the salt because both the wine and the chorizo add their own saltiness. Tuck in the thyme and bay leaf. Bake for 35 minutes, until the chicken is cooked through. Leave the lid off the whole time — this will help the liquid reduce and further brown the chicken skin — but baste the top of the chicken with the juices every so often.

3 Sprinkle with flat-leaf parsley and serve in the casserole in which it was cooked.

serves 4

4 large chicken breasts, skin removed

salt and pepper

olive oil

1 large onion, finely chopped

16 oz Greek-style yogurt

2 large eggs, beaten

2 tbsp all-purpose flour

2 oz feta cheese, crumbled

2 tbsp chopped fresh dill

leaves from 2 to 3 mint sprigs, torn

3 cloves garlic, crushed

½ cup freshly grated Parmesan cheese

I Preheat the oven to 350°F. Season the chicken breasts with salt and pepper and quickly brown them in a couple of tbsp of olive oil over medium heat — you just want a good outside color, not to cook the chicken through. Remove these and set aside. Sauté the onion in the same pan — add a little more oil if needed — until soft and just turning golden.

2 Combine the yogurt, eggs, flour, feta, dill, mint, and garlic in a large bowl and mix well.

3 Lay the onion and the chicken in the bottom of an ovenproof dish into which everything will fit snugly. Spread the yogurt mixture evenly on top and sprinkle with the Parmesan.

4 Bake for 45 minutes. The yogurt will have set, and the chicken should be cooked through.

A smart idea from the Greeks and a lovely supper dish. The chicken cooks in a golden blanket of yogurt and cheese, set to a soft custard.

. . . . . .

greek baked chicken in yogurt

chicken

This simple recipe revolutionized my cooking. There's no browning and everything's cooked together in one dish, just thrown into the oven. It's based on one in Antonio Carluccio's book, *An Invitation to Italian Cooking*, and is what home-cooking should be: chunky, rustic, and deeply savory.

· · · · · ·

chicken baked with red onions, potatoes, and rosemary

serves 4

2 red onions, each cut into 10 wedges

1¼ lbs new potatoes, not peeled

2 bulbs garlic, separated into cloves, but not peeled

salt and pepper

½ cup extra virgin olive oil

2 tbsp balsamic vinegar

about 5 sprigs rosemary

1 (4-lb) roasting chicken, cut into 8 pieces, or 8 chicken thighs, rubbed with sea salt to crisp the skin

I Preheat the oven to 400°F. Spread the vegetables and garlic in a single layer over the bottom of a huge roasting pan so that they will crisp and brown beautifully. Season with salt and pepper, pour over the oil and balsamic vinegar, and add the rosemary, leaving some sprigs whole and stripping the leaves off the rest. Toss the vegetables with your hands and tuck the chicken pieces in among them. Bake for 45 minutes, until cooked through.

2 Transfer everything to a big platter — or bring to the table in the roasting pan. Serve a green salad on the side.

and also...

with sweet potato, smoked paprika, olives, and preserved lemons

A popular and more exotic take on the above. Marinate 8 chicken thighs in ¼ cup olive oil, 1 tbsp pimenton (smoked Spanish paprika), 5 crushed garlic cloves, and the finely sliced flesh of ½ preserved lemon, plus 2 tbsp juice from the jar of lemons. Put into a roasting pan as above, with 2 lbs unpeeled sweet potatoes, cut into big chunks; 2 red onions, cut into wedges; and salt and pepper. Bake in a preheated 400°F oven for 45 minutes, until cooked through, adding a handful of pitted black olives and the shredded zest of the lemon 15 minutes before the end. Sprinkle with chopped fresh parsley and mint or cilantro and serve.

We finish on the stove with this recipe for a change. As long as you find thin-skinned oranges, you actually can eat the wedges. Serve with Greek-style yogurt and rice.

• • • • • •

turkish chicken with oranges and warm spices

serves 4

1 tbsp unsalted butter

1 tbsp olive oil

8 chicken thighs, seasoned with salt and pepper

2 red onions, halved and cut into wedges

2 thin-skinned oranges, unpeeled, each cut into 8 wedges

5 cloves garlic, crushed

1 small fresh red chile, halved, seeded, and finely chopped

1 tbsp ground coriander

1 cinnamon stick

½ cup raisins, soaked in boiled water for 30 minutes and drained

juice of 1 orange

⅔ cup chicken stock

1½ tbsp thyme honey or other honey

salt and pepper

a small handful of mint leaves

I Heat the butter and oil over medium heat in a shallow casserole and brown the chicken thighs on each side. Lift out the chicken and set aside. Add the onions and oranges to the pan and sauté for 2 to 3 minutes. Add the garlic, chile, dried spices, and raisins and cook for another 2 to 3 minutes. Pour in the orange juice, stock, and honey. Season with salt and pepper and simmer for 10 minutes.

2 Return the chicken to the pan, cover, and cook over low heat for 20 to 25 minutes, until the chicken is cooked through. Check the seasoning, sprinkle the mint over the top, and serve.

and also...

spanish chicken with sherry and pine nuts

Brown chicken thighs as above, then add ⅔ cup soaked raisins and 1¼ cups medium sherry. Cover and simmer over low heat for 20 to 25 minutes, until cooked. Sprinkle with 3 tbsp toasted pine nuts and chopped fresh parsley.

There's nothing like charred meat, herbs, and the crunch of sea salt to get the juices flowing. Thighs have a much better flavor and texture for grilling than chicken breasts.

• • • • • •

grilled chicken with thyme and sea salt

serves 4

8 boneless chicken thighs, skin on, opened out flat

¼ cup olive oil

chopped leaves from about 10 sprigs thyme

sea salt and pepper

juice of 1 lemon

lemon wedges, to serve

I With a very sharp knife, make some slits in the chicken thighs on both sides. Rub them with the olive oil and pat on the thyme leaves. Cover and leave to marinate in the refrigerator overnight, or for a couple of hours.

2 Heat a grill pan until it is really hot. Season the oiled and herbed chicken with sea salt and pepper and put it onto the grill pan, skin-side down. Let it sizzle and splatter for 2 minutes. Turn the chicken over and let it cook for another 2 minutes. Lower the heat and continue to cook until the thighs are done all the way through — about another 5 minutes — turning once more.

3 Pour on the lemon juice and serve immediately with lemon wedges.

and also...

with cilantro and chile butter
Marinate the chicken in olive oil as above (omit the thyme), then mix ⅓ cup softened unsalted butter with the shredded flesh of 2 medium fresh red chiles (halved and seeded), a handful of fresh cilantro leaves, 1 fat crushed garlic clove, and a good squeeze of lime. Put the butter in the refrigerator to get really cold. Grill the chicken as above and serve with a pat of butter melting over the top and some wedges of lime.

with black olive and anchovy butter
Again, marinate the chicken in olive oil as in the first recipe (omit the thyme), then mash together ⅓ cup softened unsalted butter with 3 chopped anchovy fillets, 1 crushed garlic clove, pepper, a good squeeze of lemon juice, and 2 tbsp chopped pitted black olives. Refrigerate. Grill the chicken as above and serve knobs of the butter melting over it.

chicken

17

Spanish rice dishes, such as this, are a real boon for the tired cook. Unlike risottos, you can just leave them to look after themselves — you must *not* stir them.

· · · · · ·

arroz con pollo y chorizo

serves 6

½ cup extra virgin olive oil, plus more as needed

12 chicken thighs, bone in, skin on

salt and pepper

2 red bell peppers, seeded and sliced

8 oz Spanish chorizo, cut into small chunks

1 large onion, coarsely chopped

4 cloves garlic, crushed

1 tbsp pimenton (smoked Spanish paprika)

1 tsp dried red pepper flakes

5¼ cups chicken stock

2 cups Spanish paella rice (Calasparra or Valencia)

2 tbsp chopped fresh flat-leaf parsley

juice of 1 lemon

and also...

caribbean lazy chicken and rice

This was given to me by food writer Richard Cawley. As long as you don't overdo the hot sauce, children love it. Marinate 8 chicken thighs with 4 crushed garlic cloves, the juice of a lime, leaves from 4 sprigs thyme, and ½ tbsp West Indian hot sauce (or other hot sauce). Wash 1 cup basmati rice until the water runs clear, then combine the rice, 1 chopped onion, and 6 oz sliced mushrooms in a shallow ovenproof dish. Lay the marinated chicken on top in a single layer and pour on the marinade. Season well with salt and pepper and pour on 2½ cups hot chicken stock. Cook, uncovered, for 45 minutes in an oven preheated to 400°F until cooked through. A spinach and avocado salad is good alongside.

I Heat the olive oil in a broad shallow pan, season the chicken thighs with salt and pepper, and brown on all sides. Take the chicken out of the pan and set aside. Add the bell peppers and chorizo to the same pan and sauté over medium heat until the peppers soften. Throw in the onion and garlic and cook until the onion is soft. Stir in the paprika and red pepper flakes and cook for a minute, then add the chicken stock. Return the chicken pieces to the pan, and simmer, covered, over low heat for 15 minutes.

2 Preheat the oven to 350°F. Most people don't have a pan big enough to fit all the chicken in a single layer and still have room for the rice, so transfer the chicken, vegetables, and stock to a big, wide ovenproof dish — the one I use for this is 13 inches in diameter. Pour the rice around the chicken and season really well with salt and pepper. Bake for 20 minutes, until the stock has been absorbed and the top is golden. When cooked, cover the dish with aluminum foil and leave for 5 minutes. Sprinkle with parsley and drizzle with lemon juice and olive oil to serve.

Small effort, big flavor, and big impact. Serve on a bed of couscous (see the recipe on page 189; the more jeweled the better) and sing "Marrakesh Express" (or "Midnight at the Oasis" or something similar) as you carry it to the table.

• • • • • •

north african spiced poussins

serves 4

8 tsp coriander seeds
8 tsp cumin seeds
8 tsp harissa
½ cup olive oil
salt and pepper
4 poussins
cilantro and mint leaves, olive oil, and lemon, to serve

I Preheat the oven to 400°F. Dry-fry the coriander and cumin seeds in a small frying pan for a couple of minutes, just to release their fragrance. Grind them in a mortar and pestle and add the harissa, olive oil, salt, and pepper.

2 Season the inside of the birds with salt and pepper and paint the spice paste onto the skin. Roast for 45 to 50 minutes, until the poussins are cooked through.

and also...

poussins with gremolata, pasta, and peas

Preheat the oven to 400°F. Rub 4 poussins all over with about ¼ cup softened unsalted butter and season with salt and pepper. Roast for 45 to 50 minutes. Check for doneness. Finely chop the zest of 1 lemon and mix with 2 finely chopped garlic cloves and a good handful of finely chopped flat-leaf parsley. Sprinkle this gremolata over the poussins and serve with cooked small pasta shapes that you've mixed with cooked peas, seasoning, and a good slug of extra virgin olive oil.

poussins with lemon, orange, and oregano

Mix together the zest of 1 orange and 1 lemon, the juice of 4 oranges and 1 lemon, 6 tbsp balsamic vinegar, ½ cup olive oil, 6 crushed garlic cloves, and 3 tbsp dried oregano. Marinate the poussins in this, covered, for a couple of hours or overnight in the refrigerator, turning them every so often. Season and put in a roasting pan with 3 oranges and 2 lemons cut into wedges (drizzle the fruit with a little olive oil and season with salt and pepper) and roast as above. Spoon the marinade over the birds every so often during the roasting. When cooked, remove the poussins and boil the cooking juices to thicken them. Serve the poussins with the reduced juices and charred wedges of fruit.

It's a pity we think of stuffings mainly as accompaniments to turkey. They're a great way to turn plain roasts into something special, and the most inexperienced of cooks can make them. These recipes give you enough to stuff a 4-pound chicken or boned leg of lamb, or 4 poussins.

· · · · · ·

lots of ideas for stuffings

All of these should be stuffed into the cavity of a bird or inside a boned leg of lamb before cooking. If you prefer not to stuff poultry, bake the stuffing alongside the meat, covered with aluminum foil for 30 minutes, then remove the foil, and bake for another 10 minutes.

chorizo, red pepper, and potato stuffing

Sauté 6 oz sliced chorizo (pull the papery skin off first) with a seeded and chopped red bell pepper and 2 tbsp olive oil. Add 8 oz finely cubed waxy potatoes (don't worry about peeling them) and cook for another couple of minutes, until the potato is pale gold and the pepper is quite soft. Season with salt and pepper and add some chopped fresh parsley or cilantro and a squeeze of lemon. Let the stuffing cool. Good for chicken or poussins.

potato, olive, fennel, and pancetta stuffing

Remove any tough outer leaves from 2 fennel bulbs. Trim at the top and bottom, quarter the bulbs, and remove the core. Discard these bits but keep any little fronds of fennel to add to the final stuffing. Chop the fennel bulb, then sauté it in 3 tbsp olive oil with 8 oz finely cubed waxy potatoes (no need to peel them); ½ small onion, finely chopped; ¼ cup chopped black olives; and 4 oz finely cubed pancetta. Add the grated zest of ½ lemon, season with salt and pepper, and leave to cool. Use to stuff chicken, poussins, or boned leg of lamb.

watercress, apricot, and hazelnut stuffing

An idea shamelessly stolen — and little changed — from the wonderful chef Shaun Hill. Sauté a finely chopped onion in 2 tbsp salted butter. Finely chop ½ cup dried apricots and mix into the butter with 1 cup whole-wheat bread crumbs; ½ cup halved, toasted hazelnuts; and 2 oz chopped watercress leaves. Season with salt and pepper, then add 2 tbsp butter, cut into little chunks, and 1 beaten large egg. Combine everything well. Use to stuff chicken or poussins.

georgian stuffing

Gorgeous and exotic. Mix ⅔ cup walnut pieces with 8 oz crumbled feta cheese, 3 crushed garlic cloves, the seeds from ½ ripe pomegranate (see page 104), a handful of chopped fresh cilantro, ¼ cup olive oil, and salt and pepper. Stuff a chicken or poussins with this, drizzle with olive oil, and sprinkle on salt, pepper, and ground cayenne. Roast and serve with wedges of lemon, a green salad, and a big bowl of bulgur wheat. You can also use dried sour cherries — soaked and drained — in place of the pomegranate seeds.

fruited couscous stuffing

Pour ½ cup boiling water or stock over ⅔ cup couscous and leave for 15 minutes. Fork through the

grains to separate them, add 2 tbsp of olive oil, and season well with salt and pepper. Stir in ⅔ cup chopped dried fruit (soaked and drained — raisins, apricots, cherries, and cranberries are all good) and the grated zest and juice of ½ lemon. The shredded rind of ½ preserved lemon is good too, and you can add chopped pistachios or almonds as well, plus chopped fresh parsley, mint, or cilantro. For chicken, poussins, or a boned leg of lamb.

prune, sausage, and brandy stuffing

Put 15 pitted and chopped prunes in a small saucepan and pour over enough brandy just to cover. Simmer over very low heat for 15 minutes. The fruit will plump up. Sauté a finely chopped onion in 2½ tbsp salted butter until soft, then add 8 oz sausage meat and cook until pale gold. Add 1 tart chopped apple (cored but not peeled), the grated zest and juice of ½ orange, ½ cup bread crumbs, a good handful of chopped fresh parsley or some thyme leaves, and season with salt and pepper. Mix and add the prunes and their soaking liquid. Leave to cool. For chicken or poussins.

aliza's chestnut, cranberry, and oat stuffing

Don't just use this at Christmas or Thanksgiving — it's too good. Sauté 1 coarsely chopped small onion in ⅓ cup salted butter until soft but not colored. (You can also sauté finely cubed pancetta or bacon, or chunks of sausage meat with the onion.) Add ¾ cup fresh cranberries and cook until they have softened, then add ½ cup dried cranberries and 4 heaping tbsp cranberry sauce or jelly. Stir until the jelly has melted, then add ⅔ cup old-fashioned rolled oats and 1 cup cooked vacuum-packed chestnuts (coarsely chopped) and season really well with salt and pepper. Stir. The mixture should be quite moist and shiny — add more butter if it isn't. Leave to cool. Use to stuff chicken or poussins.

eggplant and date stuffing

One for using to stuff boned lamb. You could serve tahini dressing (see page 118) on the side, or a bowl of yogurt seasoned with some chopped fresh mint and crushed garlic. Cut an eggplant into small cubes and sauté in a frying pan in 3 tbsp olive oil until golden on all sides. Season and put into a bowl. Using another 2 tbsp olive oil, sauté ½ onion, finely chopped, until soft but not colored. Add a crushed garlic clove and 1 tsp ground cinnamon and cook for another minute. Stir into the eggplant along with 1 cup chopped pitted dates, the juice of ½ lemon, salt and pepper, and 12 torn mint leaves.

cherry and dill stuffing

Scandinavian-inspired and lovely with chicken in the spring. Sauté a finely chopped onion in ¼ cup salted butter until soft but not colored. Mix this into 1½ cups white bread crumbs, 3 oz chopped watercress (leaves and fine stems only), and ¾ cup dried pitted sour cherries that have been soaked in boiling water for 15 minutes and drained. Add a beaten large egg, chopped leaves from a small bunch of dill, salt, and pepper. Eat your stuffed chicken with a bowl of sour cream mixed with chopped cucumber and a crushed clove of garlic.

polish stuffing

Melt 3 tbsp salted butter in a frying pan and cook a small finely chopped onion until soft but not colored. Add 4 oz finely chopped chicken livers and cook for a few more minutes. Put into a bowl with 4 oz good cooked ham, chopped; 3 cups white bread crumbs; 4 tbsp chopped fresh dill; 1 small beaten egg; and salt and pepper. Mix everything together. Use to stuff a chicken and serve with baked red beets (see page 126), drizzled with a little buttermilk or daubed with sour cream.

chops

This is good for a sunny spring or summer evening. I'm a big fan of frozen peas: they're sweet, a fantastic color, and, since they are frozen so soon after picking, often taste better than ones you buy and shell yourself. You can use basil or cilantro leaves instead of mint; the results are just very different.

. . . . . .

lamb chops with pea and mint puree

and also...

with ligurian fava bean puree

Cook 1 lb shelled fava beans (fresh or frozen) in boiling water until tender. Drain and, if you have the time, slip the skins off the beans; if you don't, just leave them on and you'll have a rougher puree. Put the beans in a food processor with 2 garlic cloves, 12 mint leaves, 5 anchovy fillets, and ¼ cup freshly grated pecorino cheese. Using the pulse button, make a rough puree while adding 10 tbsp extra virgin olive oil. Add the juice of ½ lemon, taste, season with salt and pepper, and blend again. Cook the lamb chops as above and serve with the puree, which can be warm or at room temperature. This puree is also good with grilled chicken or just on rounds of grilled ciabatta.

serves 4

pea puree

8 oz fresh baby or frozen petite peas

¼ cup salted butter

1 tbsp heavy cream

salt and pepper

about 8 mint leaves

a squeeze of lemon juice

8 to 12 lamb cutlets (the number depends on size and hunger)

olive oil

salt and pepper

wedges of lemon and/or fresh mint, to serve

I Cook the peas in boiling water until tender, then drain. Add the butter and let it melt, then transfer the peas into a blender or food processor. Add the cream, salt and pepper, mint, and lemon juice and blend until smooth. You can make the puree in advance and heat it again at the last minute.

2 Heat a ridged grill pan or a frying pan for the chops. If you're going to grill them, brush them with olive oil and season with salt and pepper; if you're going to use a frying pan, heat a film of oil in it and season the chops. Cook the chops over high heat until browned on both sides but still pink in the middle. I cook cutlets for about 4 minutes in all, but I do like them rare. You can cut into the flesh of one side to see whether they're done the way you like them.

3 Serve with the warm pea puree, wedges of lemon (good squeezed over the chops — has an effect like salt), and sprigs of mint.

Pomegranate molasses is a sweet-sour (though more sour than sweet) Middle Eastern syrup made from pomegranate juice. It's particularly good with lamb and makes a great sticky glaze. Fresh pomegranate seeds are guaranteed to make any simple dish exotic.

· · · · · ·

pomegranate-and-honey-glazed chops with radish and cucumber tzatziki

serves 4

marinade

2½ tbsp pomegranate molasses

10 tbsp olive oil

1½ tbsp honey

2 cloves garlic, crushed

2 tsp cayenne pepper

8 (6-oz) thick lamb chops

olive oil

salt and pepper

radish and cucumber tzatziki

20 medium radishes, very finely sliced

½ cucumber, cut into small cubes

12 oz Greek-style yogurt

2 cloves garlic, crushed

2 tbsp coarsely chopped mint leaves

2 tbsp olive oil

to serve

a small bunch of cilantro or mint leaves (about 1 oz)

extra virgin olive oil

lemon juice

seeds from ½ ripe pomegranate (see page 104)

1 Mix the marinade ingredients together. Add the chops and make sure they get well coated. Cover with plastic wrap and refrigerate for 1 to 24 hours.

2 To make the tzatziki, simply mix the radishes, cucumber, yogurt, and garlic together. Stir in the mint leaves and olive oil.

3 Heat a thin film of oil in a frying pan and cook the chops for about 3 minutes on each side. You want to get a good color on the outside but must avoid burning the honey and pomegranate mixture, so cook over medium heat.

4 Serve the chops on a bed of fresh cilantro or mint dressed lightly with extra virgin olive oil and a squeeze of lemon juice, with the tzatziki on the side. Sprinkle pomegranate seeds over the top of the tzatziki just before serving — any sooner and the seeds bleed into the yogurt — or over the chops if you prefer.

serves 4

¼ cup olive oil

finely grated zest and juice of 1 lemon

2 cloves garlic, crushed

1 tsp each of ground sweet paprika, cinnamon, cayenne pepper, cumin, coriander, and allspice

salt and pepper

8 (6-oz) thick lamb chops

salad

1 large onion, finely chopped

5 tbsp olive oil

½ cup Greek-style yogurt

⅓ cup walnut pieces

juice of 1 lime

2 cloves garlic, finely sliced

a small handful of mint leaves, chopped

10 fresh dates, pitted and finely sliced

This salad is based on an Iranian recipe in Arto der Haroutunian's inspiring book, *Middle Eastern Cookery.* Eat with warm flatbread or a bowl of couscous, rice, or bulgur wheat. A little dish of shredded preserved lemon rind is lovely with the sweetness of the lamb and dates and the acidity of the yogurt.

· · · · · ·

spiced lamb with date, walnut, and yogurt salad

1 Mix the olive oil with the lemon zest and juice, garlic, all the spices, and salt and pepper. Put the lamb chops in this and cover with plastic wrap. Marinate in the refrigerator for 2 to 24 hours, turning the chops over every so often.

2 For the salad, fry the onion gently in 2 tbsp of the olive oil, until really soft and a little golden. Stir in the yogurt, two-thirds of the walnuts, and the lime juice. Spread this in a broad shallow bowl. Heat the remaining 3 tbsp olive oil and quickly fry the garlic until just golden. Add the mint and cook for another 20 seconds or so. Drizzle this on top of the yogurt and onion mixture, then sprinkle on the dates and the remaining walnuts.

3 You can either fry the chops or cook them on a ridged grill pan. If you're using a frying pan, you need to heat a couple of tbsp of olive oil in the pan. If you're grilling them, just heat the grill pan until it's really hot and put the chops on it. Cook the chops over high heat until browned on both sides, then turn the heat down and cook further — about 3 minutes per side in all — but keep them pink and tender in the middle. Serve with the salad.

and also...

with salsa mishmish

A Middle Eastern sauce, probably Iranian in origin. Sauté a finely chopped onion in 2 tbsp olive oil until soft and golden. Add ½ tsp ground cinnamon and a 2-inch chunk of peeled fresh ginger, finely chopped. Cook for another minute or two. Add 2 cups dried apricots and 1 cup chicken stock. Simmer for about 30 minutes, or until the mixture is thick. You can either leave the texture like this or puree it. Add the juice of a lemon; I sometimes add a bit of hot pepper sauce as well. Stir in a good handful of chopped fresh mint or cilantro leaves and serve with the lamb. This sauce is also great with grilled or roasted chicken.

Harissa is a very hot Moroccan chile paste, which is quite easy to find in large supermarkets these days. You can blend the chickpeas roughly so that you are left with more of a mash than a puree if you want something to get your teeth into. Accompany with couscous or bulgur wheat, mixed with plenty of mint or flat-leaf parsley, or just serve with pieces of warm flatbread and maybe a bowl of plain yogurt.

· · · · · ·

harissa-marinated lamb with chickpea puree

serves 4

2½ tbsp harissa

3 cloves garlic, crushed

½ cup olive oil

juice of ½ lemon

a good handful of mint leaves, torn

8 (6-oz) lamb chops, preferably from the top of the leg

salt

chickpea puree

1 (14-oz) can chickpeas, drained

¾ cup olive oil, plus extra if frying the onions

juice of 1 lemon

1 clove garlic, crushed

½ tsp cayenne pepper

1 tsp ground cumin

salt and pepper

1 onion, coarsely chopped (optional)

2 tbsp chopped cilantro leaves

I Mix the harissa with the garlic, oil, lemon juice, and mint and put the chops into it, turning them over to make sure they get well coated. Cover and put them in the refrigerator. Leave them to marinate for 1½ hours to overnight, turning them every so often.

2 To make the chickpea puree, simply chuck everything (except the onion and cilantro) into the food processor, with salt and pepper to taste, and blend. The mixture doesn't have to be absolutely smooth. If you can be bothered, fry the chopped onion in a little olive oil until golden brown and slightly singed in some parts. Sprinkle the onion and the cilantro over the puree.

3 Heat a grill pan for the chops. Salt the chops at the last minute and then cook them over high heat for about 3 minutes on each side, until browned but still pink in the middle. You can pierce the flesh to see whether they're done the way you like them.

4 Serve with the chickpea puree.

A really warming, rustic autumn or winter dish. You can use either waxy or baking potatoes in this — each will give a different result. Slices of baking potato will disintegrate, but waxy ones will remain intact. If you can't be bothered to make the butter, just serve the dish as it is with a jar of mustard on the side, and put sprigs of thyme in to bake with the chops.

· · · · · · ·

smothered pork chops with mustard and thyme butter

serves 4

mustard and thyme butter

¼ cup unsalted butter, softened

2½ tsp coarse-grain mustard

leaves from 4 sprigs thyme

1 tart apple

8 oz potatoes, washed (no need to peel them)

1 onion, thinly sliced

salt and pepper

¼ cup unsalted butter

4 (8-oz) thick pork chops, bone in and partly trimmed of fat

1¼ cups dry white wine or hard cider

I To make the mustard and thyme butter, just mash the ingredients together, form into a sausage shape, wrap in plastic wrap or parchment paper, and chill.

2 Preheat the oven to 350°F. Halve and core the apple and cut it into wedges about 1 inch thick at the thickest part. Slice the potatoes into rounds about ⅛ inch thick. Toss the potatoes with half the apple and half the onion, and season with salt and pepper. Put in the bottom of an ovenproof dish (which will take the chops in a single layer). Dot with half the butter.

3 Melt the rest of the butter in a frying pan. Season the pork chops with salt and pepper and quickly brown them on both sides (you just want to color the meat, not cook it through). Put the chops on top of the vegetables and apple and put the rest of the apple and onion on top. Deglaze the frying pan with the wine by pouring it into the pan and letting it bubble while you scrape the juices that have stuck to the pan. Pour this over the chops. Bake for 45 minutes, turning the onions and apples occasionally so that they get a good all-over color, until cooked through. Serve a couple of slices of the flavored butter on top of each helping.

This Lyon specialty is usually made with chicken parts, but onions and crunchy bread crumbs are a winning combination with pork too. Serve with a green salad and roasted potatoes.

• • • • • •

pork chops lyonnaise

serves 4

4 (8-oz) pork chops, bone in and partly trimmed of fat

salt and pepper

3 tbsp unsalted butter

2 medium onions, finely chopped

1½ tbsp Dijon mustard

leaves from 6 sprigs thyme

1 cup fresh bread crumbs

I Preheat the oven to 375°F. Season the chops on both sides with salt and pepper. Melt 1 tbsp of the butter in a frying pan and quickly brown the chops, taking care not to burn the butter. Transfer the chops to a shallow ovenproof dish.

2 Sauté the onions in the rest of the butter over very low heat for about 15 minutes, until they're really soft but not colored. Stir in the mustard and thyme.

3 Spread the onion mixture thickly over each chop and press the bread crumbs down on top of that. Bake for 35 minutes, or until cooked through, and serve.

Old-fashioned, calorific, and just what you need on a winter night. Mature cheddar will do, though it doesn't have the same elasticity as melted Gruyère. If you don't have Marsala, try a dry sherry.

• • • • • •

pork with cheese and marsala

serves 2

6 tbsp olive oil

2 (6-oz) boneless pork chops, partly trimmed of fat

salt and pepper

1 tbsp salted butter

1 medium onion, finely chopped

2 slices prosciutto

3 oz Gruyère cheese, grated

10 tbsp dry Marsala

1½ tsp finely chopped fresh flat-leaf parsley

I Heat the oil in a frying pan. Season the chops with salt and pepper and cook for 5 minutes on each side. Take them out of the pan, add the butter to the pan, and sauté the onion.

2 Lay a slice of prosciutto on each chop and top with the Gruyère. Cook under a very hot broiler for 2 to 3 minutes, until the cheese bubbles and the chops are cooked through. Meanwhile, stir the Marsala into the onion and let it bubble away to form enough slightly syrupy sauce to pour around both chops. Sprinkle with parsley and serve.

I love this dish for its utter plainness. There is something very satisfying about eating a soy-infused bit of pork with nothing more than the zap of lime and fish sauce. You don't really "dip" the pork in the sauce, but rather spoon it over. Serve with plain white rice.

. . . . . .

thai-spiced pork chops with lime dipping sauce

serves 4

6 tbsp sweet soy sauce or Kecap manis (available in large Asian markets)

salt and pepper

a handful of cilantro stems, finely chopped (keep the leaves for serving)

4 (6- to 8-oz) boneless pork chops, partly trimmed of fat

lime dipping sauce

½ cup fish sauce

juice of 2 limes

3 shallots, thinly sliced lengthwise

1 medium fresh red chile, halved, seeded, and thinly sliced

about 2 tbsp coarsely chopped cilantro leaves

I Mix the sweet soy sauce, salt, pepper, and cilantro stems in a shallow bowl and add the pork chops. Turn the chops over to make sure they get well coated. Cover loosely with plastic wrap and put in the refrigerator to marinate, preferably overnight. If you can, turn the chops over in the marinade every so often.

2 To make the lime dipping sauce, just mix everything together. Put in a small bowl to serve at the table.

3 Heat a ridged grill pan and cook the chops over high heat for 2 minutes on each side to get a good color, then turn the heat down to medium and cook for about 5 minutes on each side. Check to see that the chops are cooked by piercing the underside (the side you will put on your plate) with a sharp knife and having a look. The meat should be tender but not pink.

4 Serve with the reserved cilantro leaves and the lime dressing.

Go to a good butcher and buy thickly cut chops that are organic, or at least from pasture-raised pigs. If the butcher sells pork from heritage breeds, even better.

Despite its simplicity, this dish looks so lovely — glossy with honey, crimson juices running out of the plums — that it's special enough to serve to friends. So much better than "dinner-party" food. Serve with rice and stir-fried greens or a watercress or spinach salad.

• • • • • •

pork chops with plums and chinese spices

serves 4

1 lb plums, preferably crimson-fleshed ones

4 (8-oz) pork chops, bone in and partly trimmed of fat

5 tbsp honey

1 tsp Chinese five-spice powder

1 tsp ground ginger

1 medium fresh red chile, seeded and finely chopped

4 cloves garlic, crushed

juice of ½ orange

1 tsp white wine vinegar

salt and pepper

I Preheat the oven to 375°F. Halve and pit the plums. If they are quite large, cut them into quarters or sixths; small ones need only be halved. Lay the chops in a shallow ovenproof dish and tuck the plums in around them where they can lie in a single layer without overlapping.

2 Mix together the honey, five-spice powder, ginger, chile, garlic, orange juice, vinegar, and salt and pepper. Pour over the chops and plums, turning everything to make sure all are well coated. Bake for 45 minutes, until cooked through. Serve hot.

If you want to do a bit more with this dish, add some rinsed green olives to the pan about 10 minutes before the end of the cooking time.

· · · · · ·

spanish pork chops with orange

serves 4

3 tbsp olive oil

4 (8-oz) pork chops, bone in and partly trimmed of fat

salt and pepper

2 onions, finely chopped

½ cup sherry vinegar

juice and finely grated zest of 1 orange

1¼ cups medium sherry

leaves from about 8 sprigs thyme

I Heat the olive oil in a large frying pan and season the chops with salt and pepper. Cook them over high heat for about 2 minutes on each side, until golden brown. Remove from the pan and reserve.

2 Cook the onions for 10 minutes in the fat left in the pan, until golden. Add the vinegar, orange juice and zest, and sherry. Season, add most of the thyme, and bring to a boil. Return the chops to the pan, cover, and turn the heat to low. Simmer for 15 minutes, remove the lid, turn the chops over, and cook, uncovered, for another 15 minutes, until cooked through. Sprinkle with thyme and serve.

Another of those brilliant Italian dishes that is packed with flavor but requires very little preparation. Serve with fresh greens: arugula or watercress.

· · · · · ·

italian pork chops with fennel seeds

serves 4

4 (8-oz) pork chops, bone in

1 tbsp fennel seeds

1 tsp dried red pepper flakes

2½ tsp dried oregano

1½ tsp sea salt flakes

4 cloves garlic, peeled

¼ cup olive oil

I Make deep incisions along the fat of the chops to keep them from curling as they cook. Crush together the fennel seeds, pepper flakes, oregano, salt, and garlic with the oil in a mortar or a small food processor. Rub this all over the chops. Cover loosely and refrigerate for an hour or so.

2 Preheat the oven to 425°F. Heat a frying pan until it is really hot. Put in the chops and cook them for 2 minutes on each side. Transfer them to an ovenproof dish and bake for 20 minutes. Check that the chops are cooked through by piercing them — they should be tender but not pink. Serve with the cooking juices.

If you're always wondering what you can do to jazz up a plain pork chop or roasted chicken thighs, here are some answers. Sauces, salsas, and relishes that are easy to whip up — and behave well after you've made them — are great, tasty ways to dress up food.

· · · · · · ·

sauces, salsas, and relishes for chops and more

mint, almond, and honey sauce

Sicilian-inspired, though not authentic. In a blender, put ¼ cup toasted almonds, 4 garlic cloves, ⅝ cup mint leaves, 3 tbsp flat-leaf parsley (leaves only), 1 tbsp honey, the juice of 1 lemon, salt, and pepper. Puree while adding 1¼ cups extra virgin olive oil in a steady stream. Taste in case you want to adjust anything. Brilliant with lamb.

argentinian chimichurri

Argentinians eat this with steak. It's also good with roasted or grilled lamb or chicken. Into a blender, put the leaves from a really generous bunch of flat-leaf parsley, 3 garlic cloves, 3 tbsp red wine vinegar, the juice of ½ lime, 2 tbsp oregano leaves, 1 tsp each of ground cumin and pimenton (smoked Spanish paprika), and salt and pepper. Blend with ¾ cup extra virgin olive oil (a full-flavored one — perhaps Greek —

would be good here). You can add a fresh chopped red chile too (halved and seeded first) if you want more bite. Use this soon after you've made it: it's better fresh.

thai cucumber relish

Peel a cucumber and cut in half lengthwise. Scoop out the seeds with a teaspoon and discard. Cut the cucumber into thin, half-moon shaped slices. In a bowl, mix ¼ cup rice vinegar, 1 tbsp superfine sugar, a good pinch of salt, and 2 tbsp hot water. Add 1 medium fresh red chile, halved, seeded, and chopped; 1 very thinly sliced shallot; and the cucumber. Mix everything really well and leave to stand for an hour before serving. Good with grilled chicken, pork, or spicy fish cakes.

vietnamese peanut sauce (*nuoc leo*)

Heat 1 tbsp peanut oil in a frying pan and gently fry 2 chopped garlic cloves and 1 chopped medium fresh red chile (halved and seeded). When they begin to color, add ⅓ cup chopped, roasted, unsalted peanuts and stir-fry for a minute without coloring. Add ½ cup chicken stock, ¼ cup coconut milk, 1 tbsp light brown sugar, 1 tbsp hoisin sauce, and 1 tbsp Asian fish sauce. Simmer until the sauce thickens and oil appears on the surface. Great with roasted or grilled skewered chicken.

vietnamese ginger sauce (*nuoc mam gung*)

In a bowl, mix 1 tbsp Asian fish sauce and 1 tsp honey with the juice of 1 lime. Whisk in ¼ cup peanut oil, 6 tbsp grated peeled fresh ginger, and 2 fresh red chiles (halved, seeded, and finely chopped). Use as a dipping sauce for fish, pork, chicken, or duck.

vietnamese chile dipping sauce (*nuoc cham*)

In a mortar and pestle or a small food processor, pound 4 garlic cloves, 2 fresh red chiles (halved, seeded, and finely chopped), 1 tbsp superfine sugar,

the juice of 1 lime, and ¼ cup Asian fish sauce. Add 4 to 5 tbsp water (according to how strong you want it) and mix well. Good with tuna, pork, duck, and chicken.

mango and chile salsa

Cut the flesh of 1 small, peeled, ripe mango into small cubes, then mix with the juice of 2 limes, 3 chopped scallions, a handful of chopped fresh cilantro, and 1 fresh red chile, halved, seeded, and cut into fine shreds. Leave for 30 minutes while the flavors meld, but no longer or the fruit gets too soft. Serve with roasted or grilled pork, chicken, or lamb, or even seared tuna, especially if you've spiced the meat before cooking.

pineapple and mint salsa

Sister to the one above; use it in the same way. Cut 1 lb pineapple flesh into slices, then quarter each slice and remove the hard bit that goes right through the center of the pineapple. Cut the flesh into small chunks. Halve 1 medium fresh red chile, seed, and cut the flesh into slivers. Add to the pineapple along with 2 chopped scallions, 3 tbsp chopped mint leaves, the juice of 1 lime, 2 tbsp olive oil, and 1½ tsp superfine sugar. Mix together.

pico de gallo

Mexican. Halve and seed 1 lb well-flavored tomatoes and cut into ¼-inch cubes. Mix with 2 tbsp finely diced red onion; 1 medium fresh red chile, halved, seeded, and finely chopped; 2 tsp superfine sugar; 2 tbsp finely chopped fresh cilantro; juice of 1 lime; 2 tbsp beer (Mexican if possible!); salt; and pepper. Cover and chill for 30 minutes before using. Serve with chicken, pork, or steak, with sour cream and sliced avocados alongside.

creamy mustard sauce

An old-fashioned French sauce. Melt 1 tbsp salted butter in a small pan and gently sauté 4 chopped shallots until soft but not colored. Add ¼ cup white wine vinegar, turn up the heat, and boil to reduce to about 1½ tsp. Add ⅔ cup dry white wine and reduce by half, then add 1 cup heavy cream, 1½ tbsp Dijon mustard, and a squeeze of lemon. Season with salt and pepper and heat through. You want a sauce the consistency of whipping cream, so if it's too thick add a little water. Good with chicken, fish, or pork.

saffron cream sauce

Heat ⅔ cup dry white wine in a saucepan until the wine has almost evaporated. Add 1½ cups really well-flavored chicken stock and ½ tsp saffron threads. Boil until reduced by two-thirds, then add ⅓ cup heavy cream. Simmer again to reduce the sauce until it is thick enough to coat the back of a spoon. Delicious with poached white fish or sautéed chicken breast.

sauce vierge

Warm ½ cup extra virgin olive oil (preferably a fruity one from Provence) with 1 garlic clove, bashed with skin on, over a low heat. Remove from the heat and add 6 torn basil leaves and a good pinch of salt. Let the flavors infuse for about 10 minutes, then remove the flavorings. Add the finely chopped flesh of 3 peeled plum tomatoes. You can either gently reheat the oil or serve at room temperature. Add 6 torn basil leaves and maybe finely chopped pitted black olives just before serving. Great spooned over plain broiled or roasted fish.

zhug

A very hot relish from Yemen. Serve with roasted veggies or roasted or grilled chicken or lamb. It's especially good with cold Greek-style yogurt to cut its heat. Halve and seed 3 medium fresh red chiles and 2 red bird chiles and put them into a food processor with the seeds of 8 cardamom pods, 1½ tsp caraway seeds, 3 garlic cloves, and the leaves of a large bunch of fresh cilantro. Add ½ cup extra virgin olive oil with the motor running. Taste and add a really good squeeze of lemon. Add salt to taste as well.

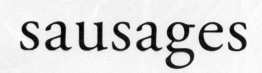

sausages

・・・・・・

I wish I had a dollar for every time I've cooked this dish. All you need to do is remember to buy sausages and broccoli on the way home from work and dinner will be on the table in 20 minutes. Dried red pepper flakes are a great thing to keep in your cupboard.

• • • • • •

italian sausages with purple-sprouting broccoli, red pepper, and penne

serves 4

8 Italian or other spicy sausages

6 tbsp olive oil

1 onion

1 lb purple-sprouting broccoli or broccoli rabe

4 cloves garlic, finely sliced

1 tsp dried red pepper flakes

1 cup dry white wine or dry vermouth

salt and pepper

8 oz penne

3 tbsp extra virgin olive oil

freshly grated Parmesan cheese, to serve

I Cut the sausages into lengths about the size of half your index finger. Heat the olive oil in a sauté pan (which has a lid) and brown the sausages all over. Scoop out the sausages and set them aside.

2 Halve the onion lengthwise, then cut each half, from tip to root, in crescent-moon-shaped slices about ½ inch thick at the thickest part. Heat the oil that is still in the pan and cook the onion over a fairly high heat until golden, but not brown. Add the broccoli and stir it around, then add the garlic and pepper flakes and cook for about a minute. Return the sausages to the pan, add the wine, season with salt and pepper, and bring to a boil. Immediately turn the heat down, cover, and leave to cook for about 7 minutes, until the broccoli is just tender, the sausages are cooked, and the cooking juices have reduced.

3 While the sausages are simmering, cook the penne in plenty of boiling salted water until al dente. Drain and immediately stir the pasta into the sausage mixture. Check the seasoning, drizzle on the extra virgin oil, and serve with freshly grated Parmesan.

You may only be cooking sausages, but the bunches of baked grapes make this dish look luxurious. This is a dish that is special enough for a supper party. Saba (or sometimes sapa) is grape must. Find it online or in specialty food stores. If you can't find it, substitute vin cotto.

· · · · · ·

vine-growers' sausages

serves 4

1 onion, sliced

2 celery stalks, finely chopped

salt and pepper

olive oil

8 good-quality pork sausages

8 oz seedless red grapes

2 bay leaves

1 cup red wine

¼ cup saba

I Preheat the oven to 375°F. Put the onion and celery in the bottom of an ovenproof dish that will hold the grapes and sausages in a single layer. Season with salt and pepper and stir in 2 tbsp olive oil. Lay the sausages and grapes on top (leave about half the grapes on their stems — it just looks nice). Using a wooden spoon, crush about a third of the grapes so that their juice comes out. Tuck in the bay leaves. Season with salt and pepper and drizzle a little olive oil over the grapes and sausages. Mix the wine with the saba and pour it around the sausages.

2 Roast for 50 minutes, until cooked through. You can turn the sausages over halfway through the cooking time so they get colored on both sides.

Sweet, sour, spicy, and very Italian, this robust dish certainly makes a hearty supper. Serve with something slightly bitter, such as grilled radicchio.

. . . . . .

salsiccia agrodolce

serves 4

3 tbsp olive oil

8 spicy sausages, preferably Italian

1 onion, coarsely chopped

⅓ cup pine nuts

2 tsp dried red pepper flakes

6 tbsp currants

2 tbsp red wine vinegar

1 tbsp sugar

2 cups chicken stock

salt and pepper

1 bay leaf and a couple of sprigs of thyme

1 tbsp coarsely chopped fresh flat-leaf parsley

2 tbsp capers, drained of brine, or washed if in salt

I Preheat the oven to 350ºF. Heat the olive oil in a large Dutch oven. Fry the sausages to brown them on all sides. Turn down the heat and add the onion. Cook gently until soft, add the pine nuts, and cook until lightly colored. Add all the other ingredients, except the capers, and bring to a boil.

2 Bake, uncovered, for 30 minutes, until the sausages are done. Stir in the capers and serve.

Find vacuum-packed chestnuts online or at specialty food stores. Their sweetness and texture lift plain dishes to greatness.

. . . . . .

baked sausages with chestnuts

serves 4

8 good-quality pork sausages

1 cup cooked vacuum-packed chestnuts

12 oz field mushrooms (or substitute button mushrooms), cut into thick slices

1 large onion, cut into half-moon-shaped wedges

1 bulb garlic, cloves separated but not peeled

⅔ cup olive oil

4 sprigs rosemary

1 bay leaf

salt and pepper

1¼ cups red wine

I Preheat the oven to 375ºF. Put everything except the red wine into a broad, shallow casserole dish. Turn the ingredients over so they become coated in olive oil.

2 Roast for 25 minutes. Pour in the wine and cook for another 25 minutes. The sausages and vegetables will cook and brown, and the wine will reduce, leaving you with a gorgeous dark and bubbling dish.

3 Serve with mashed or olive-oil-roasted potatoes, or just some bread and a salad of winter greens, such as endive, radicchio, and spinach.

¼ cup olive oil

8 oz bacon lardons or fatback

12 good-quality sausages, preferably Toulouse

1 onion, chopped

1 celery stalk, chopped

2 carrots, cut into small cubes

1 (14-oz) can tomatoes in puree

2 (14½-oz) cans cannellini beans, one drained,
the other not

1⅛ cups wine, chicken stock, or water

1 bay leaf, a small handful of parsley leaves, and the
chopped leaves from 3 sprigs thyme

2 tsp sugar

salt and pepper

1¼ cups fresh white bread crumbs

I love cassoulet, the sausage, duck confit, and bean dish beloved of Southwest France, but it takes an age to make. This is my lazy person's substitute. It never ceases to amaze me how a dish that looks totally unappetizing raw turns into this thick, dark, unctuous stew.

• • • • • •

simple gascon sausages and beans

I Preheat the oven to 350°F. Heat the oil in a frying pan and brown the lardons and sausages all over. Put them into a shallow broad casserole dish. Add everything else, except the bread crumbs, and season really well with salt and pepper. Sprinkle a third of the bread crumbs on top. Bake for 2 hours. Sprinkle on the rest of the bread crumbs in two separate batches during the cooking time. Stir in the previous sprinkling of crumbs before adding the next batch.

2 Taste the stew and adjust the seasoning toward the end of the cooking time — beans take a lot of flavoring.

and also...

spicy sausages and beans

Make as above, but add 2 fresh red chiles (halved, seeded, and chopped) and 2 tsp ground cumin. If you don't have fresh chiles, use a hot pepper sauce such as Tabasco instead. You can also use kidney beans or mixed beans. Stir a handful of cilantro leaves into the pot before serving with some wedges of lime and a bowl of sour cream on the side.

A meal you can eat with just a fork, this is perfect, comforting midweek food. Smoked paprika or pimenton is available in many specialty food stores nowadays.

. . . . . .

spanish sweet potato with chorizo, peppers, and fried egg

serves 2

2 sweet potatoes

1 red onion, halved and cut into half-moon-shaped slices

1 green bell pepper and 1 red bell pepper, seeded and sliced into wide strips

olive oil

1½ tsp pimenton (smoked Spanish paprika)

¼ tsp ground cumin

salt and pepper

8 oz chorizo, cut into thick rounds

4 oz bacon or pancetta, cut into meaty chunks

2 cloves garlic, finely chopped

1 tbsp chopped fresh cilantro or flat-leaf parsley leaves

2 large eggs

I Preheat the oven to 400°F. Cut the sweet potatoes into chunks — you don't have to peel them — and put in a small roasting pan with the onion and bell peppers. Add 2 tbsp olive oil, the pimenton, cumin, salt, and pepper. Stir the vegetables until they're coated in oil and spices. Roast for about 30 minutes, or until all the vegetables are tender and slightly charred.

2 Heat 1 tbsp olive oil in a frying pan and cook the chorizo and bacon until colored. Turn the heat down, add the garlic, and cook for another minute. Add all this to the cooked vegetables. Stir in the chopped herbs.

3 Heat a little more oil in the same frying pan and fry the eggs. Serve the sweet potato mixture topped with the fried eggs.

I really cheat with sausages: I brown them only if I have time or it's crucial to the dish, but more often than not I just stick them straight into the oven.

· · · · · ·

baked sausages with leeks, apples, and cider

serves 4

3 leeks, washed and chopped into 1-inch lengths

2 apples, halved, cored, and cut into wedges

8 good-quality pork sausages

¼ cup olive oil

salt and pepper

2 tbsp salted butter, in small pieces

1⅛ cups hard cider

2 tbsp coarse-grain mustard

I Preheat the oven to 375°F. Put the leeks and apples into an ovenproof dish and arrange the sausages in a single layer on top. Drizzle over the olive oil, season with salt and pepper, and toss everything around. Dot the top with butter and pour in the cider. Bake for 50 to 60 minutes.

2 About 10 minutes before the end of cooking time, spread the mustard over the sausages and any sticking-out apple pieces, and return to the oven.

3 Serve with creamy mashed potatoes or rosemary-roasted new potatoes.

These always go down really well, whether served in hot dog rolls or with buttery roasted onions and mashed potatoes.

· · · · · ·

honey-and-mustard-glazed sausages

serves 4

2 tbsp honey

1½ tbsp coarse-grain mustard

12 good-quality pork sausages

I Preheat the oven to 400°F. Mix the honey and mustard in a bowl. Add the sausages and turn them around in it. Put the sausages into a shallow baking dish and roast for about 25 minutes. Turn the sausages every so often and baste them with their juices. The sausages will end up glazed and sticky.

and also...

maple-and-mustard-glazed sausages
Make as above, but substitute maple syrup for honey.

If you can't find merguez sausages, use other spicy sausages but let them cook on the vegetables for 25 minutes. Regular sausages are much thicker than merguez so need longer cooking. Serve with warm flatbread or couscous.

. . . . . .

merguez sausages with roasted peppers and cucumber tzatziki

serves 6

4 bell peppers, a mixture of red and yellow

1 medium fresh red chile, halved, seeded, and sliced

1 lb plum tomatoes, halved

1 large red onion, halved and cut into crescent-shaped slices

about 5 tbsp olive oil

salt and pepper

6 sprigs thyme

12 to 16 merguez sausages

1 cup tomato puree

about 2 tbsp coarsely chopped fresh flat-leaf parsley

cucumber tzatziki

½ cucumber

2 cloves garlic, crushed

1 cup Greek-style yogurt

1½ tbsp extra virgin olive oil

2 tbsp chopped fresh mint leaves

salt and pepper

I Preheat the oven to 350°F. Cut the peppers in half, seed them, and then cut into broad slices, about ⅜ inch wide at the thickest part. Combine the peppers, chile, tomatoes, and onion with 3 tbsp of the olive oil, salt and pepper, and thyme in a wide cast-iron or stainless-steel sauté pan where they can lie pretty much in a single layer. Toss everything with your hands to make sure there's a good coating of olive oil. Roast for 40 minutes.

2 To make the tzatziki, grate the cucumber coarsely and then squeeze out the excess water by pressing the flesh in your hands. Add it to the garlic, yogurt, oil, mint, and salt and pepper. Mix well, cover, and chill until you need it.

3 Heat the remaining 2 tbsp oil in a frying pan until really hot and quickly brown the sausages on all sides. Set them aside. When the vegetables have just 15 minutes of cooking time to go, stir in the tomato puree. Season with salt and pepper and add the sausages — just set them on top — and return to the oven.

4 Serve in the dish in which it has cooked, sprinkled with parsley, accompanied by the tzatziki.

leg of
lamb
•••••••

Lamb and anchovies are a match made in heaven: the saltiness of the anchovies somehow counteracts the sweetness of the lamb and at the same time emphasizes it. The fish melt into the meat, seasoning it as they disintegrate.

You don't have to finish this off with cream — the cooking juices are good served just on their own — but it works, even though mixing anchovies and cream seems like a culinary culture clash.

• • • • • •

roast leg of lamb with anchovy cream

serves 6

1 (4-lb) leg of lamb, trimmed of excess fat

2 tbsp salted butter, slightly softened

1 (2-oz) can anchovies, drained and chopped

4 cloves garlic, peeled and crushed

freshly ground black pepper

leaves from 4 sprigs thyme

2½ cups dry vermouth

1 cup water

⅔ cup heavy cream

1 Preheat the oven to 425°F. Make deep incisions all over the leg. Mash together the butter, anchovies, garlic, pepper, and thyme. (You can blend these in a small food processor or with a mortar and pestle, or just a fork and a small bowl.) Push the butter down into the incisions.

2 Put the lamb in a roasting pan and roast for 15 minutes, then turn the heat down to 375°F and roast for 50 minutes. Pour on half the vermouth once the lamb has roasted for 20 minutes, and the rest after it has been roasting for 40 minutes.

3 Transfer the lamb to a hot platter, cover with aluminum foil, insulate it (I use some kitchen towels), and leave to rest for 15 minutes.

4 Add the water to the roasting pan and set it over high heat. Dislodge the cooking juices from the pan using a wooden spoon — you want to get all the flavor in the pan. Boil the cooking juices until they have reduced by a third, then add the cream. Boil again until you have a slightly syrupy sauce. Serve the lamb with the sauce.

1 (4-lb) leg of lamb, trimmed of excess fat

2 fat cloves garlic, cut into slivers

2 sprigs thyme

¼ cup salted butter, slightly softened

salt and pepper

1 cup hard cider

a good slug of Calvados or brandy

2⅓ cups chicken or lamb stock

¾ cup crème fraîche

We so often partner lamb with Mediterranean flavors — tomatoes and olives, for example — that it's good to find a dish from an area famed for its lamb and dairy produce. Serve this with flageolet or cannellini beans heated with a generous pat of butter, salt and pepper, a squeeze of lemon, and a handful of chopped parsley. Put the lamb on a warm platter, spoon the parsleyed beans around it, and you'll be off looking for your Jacques Brel CD.

· · · · · ·

normandy roast lamb with cider

I Preheat the oven to 425°F. Make small incisions all over the leg and stuff each hole with a sliver of garlic and a little bit of thyme. Rub the butter over the roast, stuffing some of it down inside the incisions, then season really well with salt and pepper. Roast for 15 minutes, then turn the heat down to 375°F and roast for another 50 minutes.

2 Put the lamb on a heated platter, cover with aluminum foil, then cover with kitchen towels to insulate it so that the roast can rest for 15 minutes.

3 Pour the roasting juices into a pitcher and skim off the fat. Set the roasting pan over medium heat and deglaze the pan with the cider and Calvados. Boil until the liquid is reduced by two-thirds, then add the stock and cooking juices. Boil until this is reduced by two-thirds, then add the crème fraîche. Boil until slightly syrupy. Serve the lamb on a heated platter with the sauce in a warm gravy boat.

Goat cheese is delicious with lamb, so try other stuffings based on it — one with soaked dried figs, walnuts, and goat cheese is excellent, for example. Though saltier and less creamy, feta is a good substitute for goat cheese.

. . . . . .

lamb stuffed with goat cheese, tomatoes, and basil

serves 4

stuffing

6 oz soft goat cheese, crumbled

6 oz sun-dried tomatoes packed in oil, drained, and coarsely chopped

2 oz (about ¾ cup) basil leaves, torn

1 clove garlic, crushed

3 tbsp olive oil

1 (3-lb) boneless leg of lamb, trimmed of excess fat

salt and pepper

1 Mix everything for the stuffing together gently — break up the goat cheese but don't turn it into a paste.

2 Preheat the oven to 400°F. Open the lamb out like a book. Cut some pockets in the thickest parts of the meat — this just gives you extra places into which to stuff the cheese mixture. Season the flesh of the lamb with salt and pepper and spread the stuffing over it, pushing the cheese mixture into any pockets you've created. Roll up, tie with string at intervals, and season well.

3 Place in a roasting pan and roast for 15 minutes. Decrease the temperature to 375°F and roast for another 50 minutes. Transfer the lamb to a carving board, cover with aluminum foil, and insulate with clean kitchen towels. Let rest for 15 minutes before slicing.

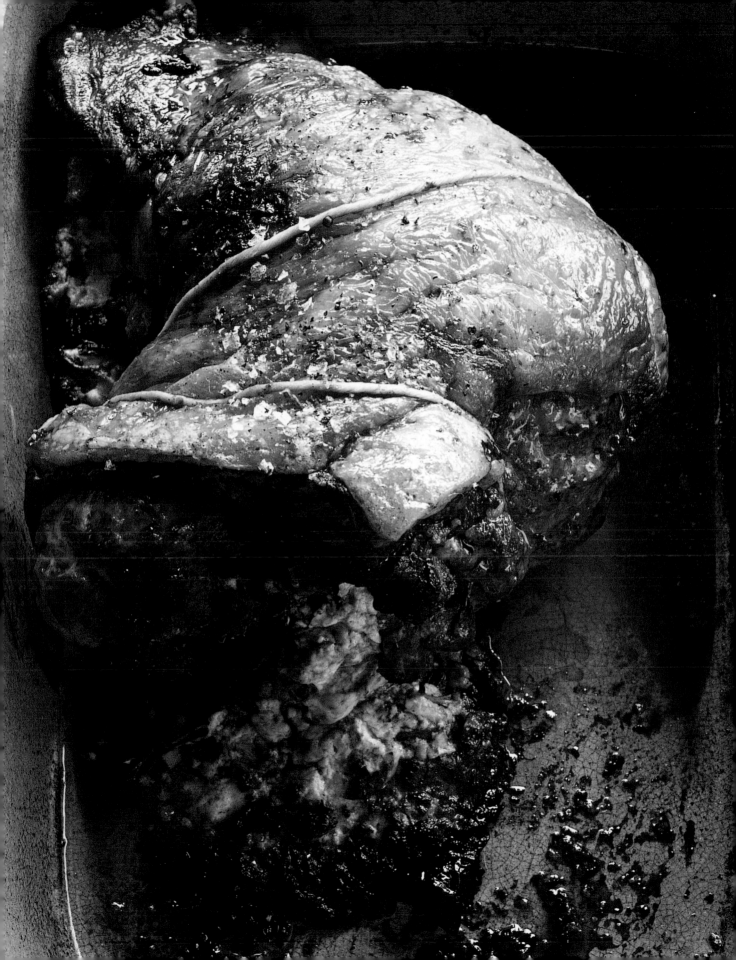

Nothing more than slightly fancy roast lamb, but the embellishments make all the difference. Serve with the cooking juices, roasted potatoes, and green salad.

• • • • • •

roast lamb with prosciutto and garlic

serves 6

1 (4-lb) leg of lamb, trimmed of excess fat

about 16 cloves garlic, cut into slivers

16 small sprigs rosemary

6 slices prosciutto, cut into 1-inch strips

olive oil

¼ cup balsamic vinegar

⅔ cup dry white wine

I Preheat the oven to 425ºF. Make incisions all over the leg. Roll a sliver of garlic and a small sprig of rosemary up in a bit of prosciutto. As you make each little bundle, stuff it into an incision in the lamb. Use up all the prosciutto, then stuff the rest of the incisions with the remaining garlic and rosemary. Push the flavorings well into the meat.

2 Season the roast with salt and pepper and rub olive oil all over it. Put in a roasting pan and pour the balsamic vinegar and wine over it. Roast for 15 minutes, then decrease to 375ºF and roast for 50 minutes, basting every so often. When the lamb is ready, let it rest, insulating it well, for 15 minutes.

The delicious cooking juices from this recipe mean you don't need to make gravy. Tie the lamb with kitchen string to hold it in shape while it cooks.

• • • • • •

sweet herbed ginger roast lamb

serves 4 to 6

1 (3-lb) boneless leg of lamb, trimmed of excess fat

leaves from 2 sprigs rosemary, chopped

leaves from 4 sprigs thyme

grated zest of ½ lemon and juice of 1 lemon

4 cloves garlic, crushed

1-inch piece fresh ginger, peeled and grated

¼ cup each honey and olive oil

3 tbsp salted butter, softened

I Open the leg of lamb so that it lies like a book. Make small incisions all over. Puree the herbs, lemon zest and juice, garlic, ginger, honey, and oil. Reserve 3 tbsp and mix the butter with the rest. Rub the butter mixture over the meat, pushing it into the slits. Re-form the leg and rub with the herb mixture. Cover loosely with plastic wrap and refrigerate for 2 to 24 hours. Bring to room temperature before roasting.

2 Preheat the oven to 425ºF. Roast for 15 minutes, then decrease to 350ºF and roast for 1 hour. Leave to rest for 15 minutes covered with aluminum foil and kitchen towels.

Cook this in a dish that you can take to the table. I sometimes sprinkle the rice with crumbled feta before serving. Roasted tomatoes are good on the side.

. . . . . .

greek roast lamb on rice and spinach

serves 6

6 tbsp olive oil

12 oz scallions, trimmed and chopped

4 cloves garlic, sliced

1 tbsp sweet paprika

2¼ lbs spinach, tough stems removed, leaves chopped

1¼ cups basmati rice

a large bunch of mint, leaves only, torn

salt and pepper

1 (4-lb) leg of lamb, trimmed of excess fat

1¾ cups chicken or lamb stock

1¾ cups dry white wine

juice of ½ lemon

4 oz feta cheese, crumbled (optional)

1 Preheat the oven to 450°F. Heat 3 tbsp of the olive oil in a large frying pan and cook the scallions until soft and wilted, about 7 minutes. Add the garlic and paprika and cook for another 2 minutes, then scrape into a bowl. Heat the rest of the oil in the same pan and cook the spinach in batches until it wilts. Add each batch to the scallions. Put the rice in the pan with the last load of spinach and turn it over in the oil for a couple of minutes so that it becomes glossy. Add this to the bowl along with the mint and season well with salt and pepper.

2 Put the lamb in a roasting pan or large shallow casserole dish and season well with salt and pepper. Roast for 15 minutes. Take the lamb out and turn the oven down to 350°F. Spread the rice and spinach mixture around the lamb in the roasting pan. Bring the stock and wine to a boil and pour it over the rice. Roast for 50 minutes. Keep an eye out to make sure the rice doesn't get too dry; the stock and wine should be completely absorbed during the cooking, but you don't want that to happen too soon. Add more wine or water if needed.

3 Remove the dish from the oven, cover with aluminum foil, insulate with a couple of kitchen towels, and leave to rest for 15 minutes.

4 To serve, squeeze some lemon over the lamb and rice and sprinkle the feta over the rice.

Here, a classic Moroccan marinade, chermoula, is rubbed into a butterflied leg of lamb, which your butcher can bone for you. Roasted flat, the meat cooks quickly. Roast lamb on the table in 40 minutes — fantastic! You don't even have to make the puree: hummus or minty yogurt goes well with the lamb too.

· · · · · ·

chermoula lamb with hot pepper and carrot puree

serves 4

chermoula

6 tbsp olive oil

1½ tsp ground cumin

½ tsp ground coriander

½ tsp sweet paprika

1 medium fresh red chile, seeded and finely chopped

finely grated zest and juice of 1 lime

2 cloves garlic, crushed

leaves from 1 small bunch cilantro, chopped

a small handful of fresh flat-leaf parsley leaves, chopped

salt and pepper

1 (3-lb) butterflied leg of lamb (boned weight), trimmed of excess fat

pepper and carrot puree

2 red bell peppers, halved and seeded

¼ cup olive oil

2 tbsp red wine vinegar

salt and pepper

1 lb carrots, chopped

½ tsp cayenne pepper or paprika

2 tbsp heavy cream (optional)

1 Mix all the chermoula ingredients together. Pierce the meat all over on both sides with a sharp knife and put in a roasting pan. Pour on the chermoula and rub it all over, making sure it gets into the little cuts. Cover with plastic wrap and marinate in the refrigerator; a couple of hours is fine, overnight is better.

2 Preheat the oven to 350°F. Put the peppers in a roasting pan, drizzle with olive oil and vinegar, and season with salt and pepper. Roast for 45 minutes, until soft. Meanwhile, barely cover the carrots with water and boil on the stovetop until soft. Drain and keep the cooking liquid. Increase the oven heat to 450°F.

3 Puree the peppers and their cooking juices with the carrots and cayenne, adding enough of the carrot cooking liquid to create a smooth puree. Add the cream, if using.

4 Roast the lamb, flesh-side down, for 15 minutes. Turn the heat down to 400°F and roast for 15 minutes. Cover with aluminum foil and a couple of kitchen towels and leave to rest for 10 minutes. Carve and serve with the puree.

For proper mechoui lamb, Moroccans cook a whole lamb in a pit with butter and spices until the meat is falling off the bone — not something you can try at home, but this roast still has quite an authentic flavor. It's gorgeous with roasted Mediterranean vegetables dressed with shreds of preserved lemon. Even simpler, wrap slices of the lamb and handfuls of salad greens in warm flatbread and daub with Greek-style yogurt.

· · · · · ·

mechoui-style lamb

serves 6

1 (4½-lb) leg of lamb, trimmed of excess fat

½ cup unsalted butter, slightly softened

6 cloves garlic, crushed

2 tsp ground cumin

2 tsp cayenne pepper

2 tsp sweet paprika

salt

I Make deep incisions all over the lamb with a sharp knife. Mash the butter with the garlic, cumin, cayenne, and paprika and rub it over the lamb, pushing it well down into the holes in the meat. Loosely cover with plastic wrap, put in the refrigerator, and leave for about 8 hours, or overnight if you can. Bring to room temperature before roasting.

2 Preheat the oven to 425°F. Salt the meat well. Roast for 15 minutes, then lower the heat to 350°F. The lamb needs to cook for another 1¼ hours, slightly longer if you don't want it to be pink. (Proper mechoui lamb isn't rare.)

3 Transfer the lamb to a warm platter, cover with aluminum foil, insulate (I usually use a couple of kitchen towels for this), and leave to rest for 15 minutes. Serve the lamb on a big warm platter.

This is adapted from Madhur Jaffrey's *Indian Cookery*, the book that accompanied her first TV series back in the early 1980s. Watching it at home in Northern Ireland — where there were no Indian restaurants and the nearest thing you could get to a curry came in a packet — my family was enchanted by this exotic cuisine.

. . . . . .

indian leg of lamb

serves 6

1 (4½-lb) leg of lamb, trimmed of excess fat

¼ cup raisins, soaked in boiling water until plump, then drained

2 tbsp flaked or slivered almonds

marinade

½ cup blanched almonds

2 onions, coarsely chopped

8 cloves garlic

a big chunk of fresh ginger, peeled and coarsely chopped

4 fresh green chiles, halved and seeded

2⅓ cups plain yogurt

1 tbsp ground cumin

4 tsp ground coriander

2 tsp ground cinnamon

2 tsp garam masala

salt and pepper

I Make deep gashes all over the meat. Put it in a baking dish or roasting pan. Put everything for the marinade (be generous with the salt and pepper) into a food processor and puree. Cover the lamb with it, pushing the marinade down into the cuts in the lamb. Pour the remaining marinade over and around the meat. Cover with plastic wrap and put the lamb into the refrigerator for 24 hours. Turn it every so often if you can.

2 Let the lamb come to room temperature. Preheat the oven to 400°F. Cover the baking dish with a lid or aluminum foil and bake for 1¼ hours. Remove the covering and bake for another 30 minutes, basting the lamb a few times. Throw the raisins and the almonds over the lamb and bake for another 5 minutes.

3 Let the lamb rest for 15 minutes, covered and well insulated with aluminum foil and a couple of kitchen towels over the top. Put the lamb on a warm platter. Skim the excess oil off the top of the cooking juices, then gently reheat in the pan, but don't boil or the mixture will curdle. Pour this around the lamb or put it in a bowl or gravy boat. Serve the lamb immediately.

fish

. . . . . .

One-pot cooking seems a difficult proposition when it comes to fish because it cooks much more quickly than most ingredients. Here the vegetables are half-cooked before the fish is added. These ingredients absolutely sing of the Mediterranean.

• • • • • •

fish baked with fennel, potatoes, and vine tomatoes

serves 4

2 fennel bulbs

1¼ lbs small waxy potatoes

olive oil

salt and pepper

12 oz vine tomatoes, left on the vine

4 (10-oz) whole sea bass or porgy, gutted, trimmed, and scaled

a handful of fresh flat-leaf parsley, roughly chopped

juice of ½ lemon

1 Trim the fennel bulbs, reserving the fronds, and remove any tough outer leaves. Quarter and cut out the central core. Cut each piece into slices, about ⅛ inch thick lengthwise.

2 Preheat the oven to 375ºF. Cut the potatoes into rounds of the same thickness. Lay the fennel in a roasting pan or large ovenproof serving dish that will hold the fish in a single layer. Pour on 1 tbsp olive oil, season with salt and pepper, and turn the fennel over with your hands, making sure it's well coated. Lay the potatoes on the fennel, season, and drizzle with 2 tbsp olive oil. Set the tomatoes on top. Season the tomatoes and drizzle oil on them too. Bake for 20 minutes.

3 Meanwhile, wash the fish and cut three slashes in the flesh on each side. Season inside and out with salt and pepper and put half of the parsley in them.

4 When the vegetables have been baking for 20 minutes, lay the fish on top of the potatoes and fennel — push the tomatoes out of the way to make room — season with salt and pepper and drizzle a little oil onto each fish. Roast for another 15 minutes. The fish is cooked when the flesh near the bone is white and opaque.

5 Squeeze the lemon juice over the vegetables and fish, sprinkle on the rest of the parsley, and serve immediately.

I cook sea bass a lot. It looks lovely whole and has sweet flesh that nevertheless stands up to strong flavors.

. . . . . .

sea bass with lebanese herb sauce

serves 4

4 (10-oz) whole sea bass or porgy, gutted, trimmed, and scaled

olive oil

salt and pepper

1½ tsp each of finely chopped fresh flat-leaf parsley and cilantro

sauce

1 cup extra virgin olive oil

1 clove garlic, chopped

1 tsp superfine sugar

¼ cup lemon juice

1 tbsp coarsely chopped fresh flat-leaf parsley

1 tbsp coarsely chopped fresh mint leaves

2 tbsp coarsely chopped fresh cilantro

1 medium fresh red chile, halved, seeded, and chopped

and also...

with *salmoriglio*
Dissolve 1½ tsp salt in the juice of 2 lemons, add the chopped leaves of a small bunch of oregano, whisk in 1½ cups extra virgin olive oil and season with pepper.

with black olive, parsley, and preserved lemon relish
Mix 1⅓ cups chopped, pitted black olives; ½ preserved lemon (skin only), finely shredded; ½ finely chopped red onion; a handful of chopped fresh flat-leaf parsley; 2 finely chopped garlic cloves; ½ medium fresh red chile (seeded and chopped); juice of ½ lemon, and ½ cup extra virgin olive oil. Season with pepper and leave for half an hour so that the flavors can meld.

with turkish almond tarator
Soak 1 slice white bread in about ¼ cup milk and leave for half an hour. Puree in a food processor with 1 cup blanched almonds, 1 garlic clove, ¾ cup extra virgin olive oil, and the juice of ½ lemon. Add water if you want a thinner sauce. Season with salt and pepper.

I Preheat the oven to 400°F. Make three slashes on each side of each fish. Brush the fish inside and out with olive oil and season with salt and pepper all over. Put into an ovenproof dish or roasting pan and bake for 8 minutes. Sprinkle with the chopped parsley and cilantro. Bake for 5 minutes. The fish is cooked when the flesh near the bone is white and opaque.

2 Put all the ingredients for the sauce, except the chile, into a blender and puree. Taste for seasoning, then add the chopped chile. Serve the fish immediately with the sauce.

If you learn the cooking times for several varieties of fish, preparing them can be as easy as grilling a chop.

Sea bass is expensive, so this is a dish for a special occasion (or very dear friends). Despite its simplicity — all you do is stick a fish in the oven — it seems spectacularly luxurious when you open the foil package and smell rosemary, fish, and wine. I first ate such a dish in Mitchell Tonks's original Fishworks restaurant in Bath and loved it so much that I recreated it at home. Now it's on the menu whenever I can justify the expense. I like it with roasted potatoes and roasted tomatoes.

· · · · · ·

roast sea bass with rosemary, garlic, and chiles

serves 4

olive oil

1 (3½-lb) whole sea bass, gutted, trimmed, and scaled

salt and pepper

3 sprigs rosemary

2 dried red chiles, crumbled

2 bulbs garlic, cloves separated but not peeled

6 tbsp dry white wine

I Preheat the oven to 400°F. Lay a large piece of aluminum foil in a roasting pan or on a baking sheet — it should be big enough to come up in a "tent" around the fish — and lightly oil the center. Put the sea bass on top, season inside and out with salt and pepper, and tuck a couple of sprigs of rosemary inside. Sprinkle the chiles and the leaves from the last sprig of rosemary on top of the fish. Throw the garlic cloves around it and drizzle some olive oil over the top.

2 Pull the foil up around the fish and pour on the wine. Pull the sides of the foil together and scrunch the edges to make a tent around the fish. It must *not* be wrapped tightly in the foil because the fish needs space to steam. Bake for 30 minutes. Serve from the foil tent in which the fish has cooked.

Don't be fooled by the simplicity of this recipe. Fish baked with a crust can be really disappointing. (If you've tasted the many frozen versions you'll know what I mean.) But abundant lemon zest and chopped parsley make this crust fresh and zingy.

· · · · · ·

baked cod with a zesty crust

serves 4

2 slices white bread, with no crusts

20 sprigs fresh flat-leaf parsley

⅓ cup freshly grated Parmesan cheese

2 cloves garlic, finely chopped

finely grated zest of 1 lemon

a good squeeze of lemon juice

7 tbsp olive oil

salt and pepper

4 (8-oz) cod fillets

I Grind the bread and parsley in a food processor. Transfer to a bowl and add the cheese, garlic, lemon zest and juice, 5 tbsp of the oil, and salt and pepper.

2 Preheat the oven to 425°F. Drizzle the rest of the oil onto a baking sheet. Turn the fillets over in the oil to coat them on both sides. Pat the crumbs on top. Bake for 7 to 10 minutes, depending on the thickness of the fish. Transfer to hot plates to serve.

Frying to get a good golden color, then finishing in the oven is a hassle-free way to cook fish fillets. It's even simpler if you have a frying or sauté pan that can go in the oven. If not, just transfer the fish to a roasting pan. This dish is lovely with pea puree (page 25).

· · · · · ·

roast cod with smoked bacon

serves 2

3 tbsp olive oil

2 (8-oz) cod fillets

salt and pepper

8 oz smoked bacon

2 tbsp unsalted butter

a squeeze of lemon juice

1 tbsp finely chopped fresh flat-leaf parsley

I Preheat the oven to 425°F. Heat 2 tbsp of the olive oil in an ovenproof frying pan. Season the cod with salt and pepper and put it into the pan. Cook for about 1½ minutes, until lightly browned underneath. Turn it over and pop the pan into the oven for 7 to 10 minutes, depending on the thickness of the fillets.

2 While the fish is roasting, heat the rest of the olive oil in a small frying pan and cook the bacon until it is browned on all sides. Add the butter and melt until foaming. Add the juice and parsley. Pour over the cod. Serve immediately.

A classy dish, which succeeds because of the interplay of flavors — the sweetness of cod, the saltiness of anchovies, and the earthiness of beans. Chopped black olives can be added to the anchovy dressing (in which case add more lemon and olive oil) or replace the anchovies altogether.

· · · · · ·

roast cod with anchovies and bean puree

serves 4

beans

2 tbsp olive oil

½ onion, coarsely chopped

1 clove garlic, crushed

2 (14-oz) cans cannellini beans, drained

⅔ cup chicken stock or water

salt and pepper

¼ cup extra virgin olive oil

a good squeeze of lemon

1 (2-oz) can anchovies, drained

1 tbsp chopped fresh flat-leaf parsley

6 tbsp extra virgin olive oil

a good squeeze of lemon

2 tbsp olive oil

4 (6-oz) cod fillets

salt and pepper

I For the beans, heat the olive oil in a saucepan and gently cook the onion until it is soft but not colored. Add the garlic, beans, stock, and salt and pepper. Cook over medium heat for about 4 minutes.

2 Process the beans and the liquid in a blender or food processor with the extra virgin olive oil and the lemon juice. Taste and adjust the seasoning. You can set the puree aside to heat up later, or serve it at room temperature.

3 Chop the anchovies and parsley together and stir in the extra virgin olive oil. Add a squeeze of lemon as well. Set aside.

4 Preheat the oven to 400ºF. Heat the 2 tbsp olive oil in a nonstick frying pan over medium-high heat. Lightly season the cod with salt and pepper and cook for 2 minutes, then turn the cod over and cook for another minute. The fillets should be a nice gold color on both sides. Transfer the fillets to a roasting pan and roast for about 8 minutes; by then the fish should be opaque and cooked through, but still moist.

5 Serve the fish with the bean puree and some of the anchovy dressing spooned over the top.

serves 4

18 oz smoked haddock fillet

14 tbsp milk

8 oz tomatoes, halved

1 tbsp unsalted butter

salt and pepper

1 cup heavy cream

4 oz aged cheddar, grated

A perfect supper dish for an autumn or winter evening. Instead of the tomatoes, you can use buttered leeks, sliced and sweated for about 15 minutes, or broccoli that you've cooked until just tender; purple-sprouting broccoli is especially good. I sometimes spread a little coarse-grain mustard over the fish before adding the vegetables and cream.

· · · · · ·

scottish smokies

I Preheat the oven to 375ºF. Butter a gratin dish. Put the haddock in a pan with the milk. Bring the milk to a boil, then quickly turn the heat down to low. Cover with a lid and poach the fish for 5 minutes; it should be only just cooked. Remove the skin from the fish and transfer the fish to the gratin dish.

2 Scoop the insides from the tomatoes and discard. Cut the flesh into slices. Melt the butter in a frying pan and quickly sauté the tomatoes until they begin to soften. Season with salt and pepper. Increase the heat to reduce the tomato cooking juices — you don't want the tomatoes to be too wet.

3 Spoon the tomatoes onto the fish. Pour on the cream and top with the grated cheese. Bake for 20 minutes. Serve golden and bubbling.

A dish I first ate in Sweden, where they're fond of oily fish. If you can't get wild mushrooms, use cultivated field mushrooms rather than button mushrooms because they have a much better flavor. Cut the field mushrooms into slices about ¼ inch thick.

• • • • • •

mackerel fillets with mushrooms, parsley, and lemon

serves 4

8 (4-oz) mackerel fillets

salt and pepper

3 tbsp unsalted butter

4 oz mushrooms, preferably a mixture of fresh wild ones and shiitake or oyster

a good squeeze of lemon juice

a small handful of fresh flat-leaf parsley, finely chopped

lemon wedges, to serve

1 Season the mackerel on both sides with salt and pepper. Melt 1 tbsp of the butter in a nonstick frying pan. Fry the fillets, flesh-side down first, until golden, then carefully turn over and cook on the skin side until crisp and golden. It will take about 3 minutes on each side to cook them through. Remove and keep warm while you cook the mushrooms.

2 Cut any large mushrooms in half or quarters. Add the rest of the butter to the mackerel pan, turn the heat up, and quickly sauté the mushrooms until they are golden. Add salt, pepper, a good squeeze of lemon, and the parsley. Serve the mushrooms spooned over or beside the mackerel. Provide lemon wedges for serving.

fish

73

An utterly simple and lovely dish. To make it with fillets of mullet instead of whole fish, cook the fruit with the oil and thyme for 10 minutes, then add eight good-sized fillets and the olives and spoon some of the fruit juices and olive oil over the top. Season and cook for another 8 minutes.

· · · · · ·

greek red mullet with oranges and olives

serves 4

4 (8-oz) whole red mullet, cleaned and gutted

salt and pepper

a good handful of thyme sprigs

¼ cup olive oil, plus a little extra for drizzling

juice of ½ lemon

1 large orange (thin-skinned if possible)

4 tbsp pitted black olives

I Preheat the oven to 350°F. Season the mullet inside and out with salt and pepper and stuff some of the thyme sprigs inside the fish. Put the fish in an ovenproof dish where they can lie in a single layer.

2 Mix the olive oil with the lemon juice and the juice of ½ of the orange and pour this all over the fish. Cut the rest of the orange into thin slices, halve these and tuck them around the fish with the rest of the thyme. Season and drizzle on a little more olive oil.

3 Bake for 15 minutes. Add the black olives and put the fish back in the oven for another 10 minutes. Serve immediately.

Tuna is a very satisfying, meaty fish. If you cook it to be slightly rare in the middle, it can be ready in minutes. This tuna goes well with corn cakes, to pick up on the Mexican theme, or with olive-oil-and-garlic roasted potatoes.

• • • • • •

seared tuna with avocado salsa

serves 4

salsa

2 avocados, peeled and chopped

8 oz tomatoes, finely chopped

1 tsp ground cumin

2 cloves garlic, finely chopped

2 scallions, finely chopped

2 medium fresh red chiles, seeded and finely chopped

juice of ½ lime

2 tbsp chopped fresh cilantro

4 tbsp extra virgin olive oil

Tabasco sauce, to taste (optional)

4 thick tuna loin steaks

olive oil

salt and pepper

to serve

1 cup sour cream

fresh cilantro leaves

2 limes, halved

and also...

with capers, chile, and lemon

Cook 2 thick tuna loin steaks as in the main recipe. Keep warm while you make the dressing. Gently heat 3 tbsp extra virgin olive oil in a small frying pan. Add 2 sliced garlic cloves; a medium fresh red chile, halved, seeded, and very thinly sliced; and 2 tbsp rinsed capers. Cook for about 30 seconds over low heat. Add a handful of chopped flat-leaf parsley, the grated zest of ½ lemon, and plenty of lemon juice. Taste and season if necessary. Pour some dressing over each piece of fish and serve immediately.

with warm beans and salsa verde

Make the salsa verde by following the recipe on page 111. Heat 2 tbsp olive oil in a frying pan and sauté 1 finely sliced onion until soft but not colored. Add a crushed garlic clove and cook for another minute, then add a drained 14-oz can of cannellini beans and another 2 tbsp of olive oil. Season and let the beans heat through. Finish with a squeeze of lemon juice and a handful of chopped flat-leaf parsley. Check the seasoning. Cook 2 tuna loin steaks as in the main recipe and serve on the beans with the salsa verde.

1 Mix all the salsa ingredients together, but don't do it more than an hour ahead of serving because it discolors. Add extra hot pepper sauce if you want it to be a little spicier. Once you've made it, cover the salsa and let the flavors infuse.

2 Use a cast-iron grill pan for cooking the fish, if you've got one. Brush each piece of tuna with a little oil and season well on both sides with salt and pepper. Let the grill pan get very hot, then cook the tuna for 1½ minutes on each side so that it's still pink in the middle, like a very rare steak.

3 Serve the tuna with a generous spoonful of salsa and a dollop of sour cream alongside. Top with cilantro and add half a lime to each plate.

Make the sauce for this ahead of time if you want to, then cook the tuna at the last minute.

· · · · · ·

sicilian sweet-and-sour tuna

serves 6

10 tbsp olive oil

2 large onions, thinly sliced

3 celery stalks, very thinly sliced

¾ cup raisins, soaked in hot water and drained

¾ cup white wine vinegar

1 cup Marsala

¾ cup green olives

2 tbsp sugar

salt and pepper

6 (½-inch-thick) tuna loin steaks

1 cup mint leaves, torn into shreds

extra virgin olive oil, to serve

Tuna is a brilliant fish for meat-eaters. Quickly seared on the outside and left rare in the middle, it's as satisfying as steak, and no more difficult to cook. And you get a classy meal in minutes.

I Heat 6 tbsp of the olive oil in a sauté pan and add the onions and celery. Cook, stirring occasionally, for about 10 minutes, until the onions are golden and soft. Add the raisins, vinegar, Marsala, olives, sugar, and salt and pepper. Stir to combine, let the mixture cook for a couple of minutes, and taste for seasoning — the mixture should be sweet-sour, but you need to get the balance right and may want to adjust it by adding more vinegar or sugar.

2 Brush the tuna steaks on both sides with the rest of the olive oil and season with salt and pepper. Heat a ridged grill pan, or an ordinary frying pan, until really hot. Quickly sear the tuna on both sides so that it gets a good color. Transfer the tuna to the sauté pan and cook for a couple of minutes in the sauce. Sicilians like the tuna in this dish to be cooked through, but I still prefer it slightly raw in the middle, so cook according to your taste.

3 Add the mint leaves and serve, with a slug of extra virgin olive oil on top.

This recipe is a boon. Pick the ingredients up on the way home from work and you'll have a lovely summery dish on the table in 20 minutes. You can add herbs — chervil or parsley, for example — to the sauce, and serve it with cold salmon or roast chicken as well.

· · · · · ·

salmon en papillote with watercress sauce

serves 4

4 (8-oz) salmon fillets

salt and pepper

¼ cup salted butter, melted

½ medium onion, very thinly sliced

1 lemon

8 sprigs dill

¼ cup dry vermouth

sauce

⅔ cup fromage blanc (or substitute crème fraîche)

⅔ cup good-quality mayonnaise

3 oz (about 1 cup) watercress

salt and pepper

I Preheat the oven to 400°F. Cut out four rectangles of parchment paper. Each rectangle should be able to hold one fillet comfortably, with enough paper to fold around it generously to make a packet.

2 Season the fish well with salt and pepper. Brush the middle of each rectangle with butter and divide the onion among them. Drizzle with a little more butter, season, then put the fillets on top. Squeeze some lemon and put 2 sprigs of dill on each fillet. Sprinkle on the vermouth and divide the remaining butter among the packets.

3 To make each packet, pull the two longest sides of the parchment paper up around the salmon and fold together. Keep folding until the packet is firmly sealed at the top, but there is plenty of room around the salmon for steam to circulate. Twist the ends of each packet. Place on a baking sheet and bake for 12 minutes.

4 Make the sauce by pureeing the fromage blanc, mayonnaise, and watercress in a blender or food processor. Season with salt and pepper.

5 When the salmon is cooked, you can open the packets slightly to reveal the contents, or let the diners do this. The sauce is lovely spooned into the packet, where it mixes with the cooking juices. Serve the rest on the side.

The sauce is a classic, and is also delicious with whole baked salmon or roast chicken.

· · · · · ·

salmon fillets with sauce messine

serves 4

4 (6-oz) salmon fillets

sauce

1 tbsp salted butter

1 shallot, very finely chopped

½ tsp all-purpose flour

¾ cup heavy cream

1 tsp Dijon mustard

1½ tsp each of finely chopped parsley and chervil

leaves from 2 stems tarragon, chopped

juice of ½ lemon

salt and pepper

I Preheat the oven to 400°F. Brush a baking sheet with a little oil and lay the salmon fillets on it, skin-side down. Roast for 12 minutes.

2 Meanwhile, melt the butter in a small pan and sauté the shallot until soft. Stir in the flour and cook for a minute. Take off the heat and gradually beat in the cream. Gently bring to a boil. Add the other ingredients and simmer for 2 to 3 minutes, until you can taste the herbs. Adjust the flavor and consistency as necessary. Serve warm.

A brilliantly easy recipe, loosely adapted from a Swedish one in Mark Hix's column in *The Independent*.

· · · · · ·

baked salmon with mustard and honey

serves 4

4 (6-oz) salmon fillets

2 tbsp coarse-grain mustard

2 tbsp honey

1½ tsp chopped fresh dill

I Preheat the oven to 400°F. Brush a baking sheet with a little sunflower or peanut oil and lay the salmon fillets on it, skin-side down. Mix the mustard, honey, and dill together and spoon it over the fish.

2 Roast for 12 minutes. Serve immediately with baby new potatoes and a cucumber salad.

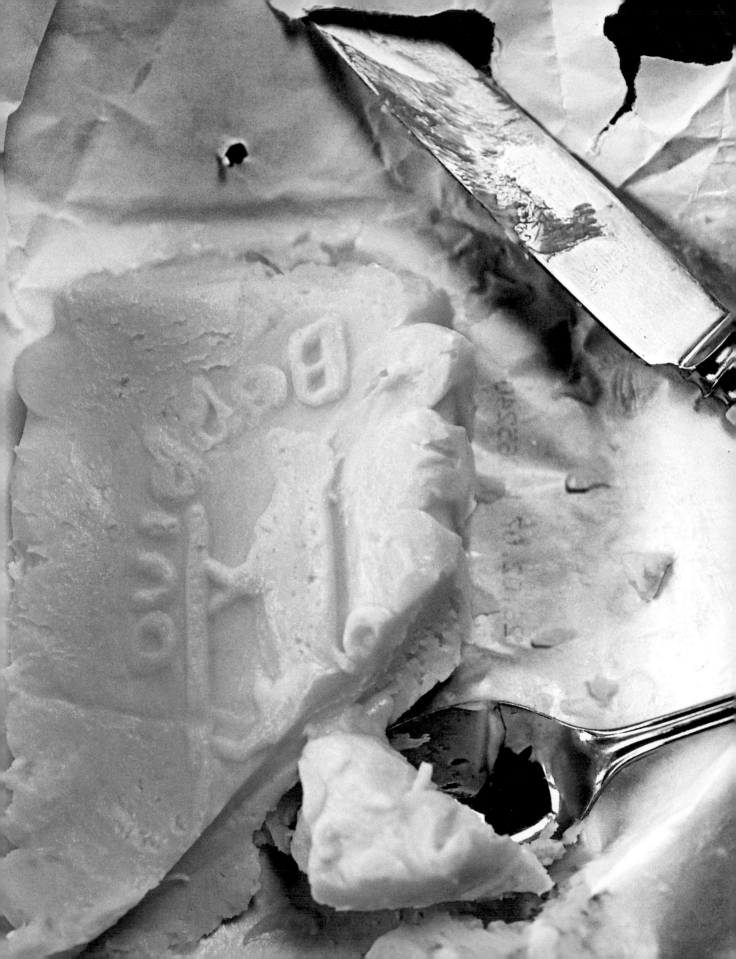

Flavored butters are probably the easiest way to dress up grilled fish and meat. Just pound the softened butter and flavorings in a mortar or beat everything together with a wooden spoon until thoroughly blended. Chill, then shape into a cylinder, and wrap in plastic wrap. Most will keep in the refrigerator for 2 to 3 days.

• • • • • •

flavored butters

herb butter
Pound 6 tbsp salted butter with 3 tbsp finely chopped herbs — a mixture of chervil, basil, parsley — until combined. Good with nearly anything grilled.

juniper and thyme butter
Pound 6 tbsp salted butter with 1 tbsp juniper berries, the juice of ½ small lemon, and the leaves from 4 sprigs of thyme. Most delicious with pork chops.

shrimp butter
Pound 6 tbsp salted butter with 2 tbsp finely chopped chervil, dill, or parsley and the juice of ½ small lemon. Finely chop 2 oz cooked shrimp and blend these in without squashing them too much. You can also replace the shrimp with chopped smoked salmon trimmings. Eat within 24 hours.

mint and cider butter
Pound 6 tbsp salted butter with 2 tbsp chopped mint, 1 tsp superfine sugar, salt, and pepper. Gradually beat in 1 tbsp cider vinegar. Serve with grilled lamb.

dill butter
Pound 6 tbsp salted butter with 2 tbsp very finely chopped dill pickles and 3 tbsp chopped fresh dill. Lovely melted over warm salmon.

martini butter
Pound 6 tbsp salted butter with 3 tbsp chopped chervil and chives, then gradually add 1 tbsp dry vermouth. Delicious with grilled Mediterranean fish.

roquefort butter
Pound 6 tbsp unsalted butter with 2 oz crumbled Roquefort. A classic with steak, but good, too, with grilled chicken.

tomato and smoked paprika butter
Pound 6 tbsp salted butter with 2 tbsp coarsely chopped oil-packed sun-dried tomatoes, 1 small crushed garlic clove, 1½ tsp pimenton (smoked Spanish paprika) and freshly ground pepper. These great Spanish flavors work best with pork, chicken, and grilled Mediterranean fish.

black olive and anchovy butter
Pound 6 tbsp unsalted butter with 3 drained, chopped anchovy fillets; 1 crushed garlic clove; and a squeeze of lemon juice. Carefully mix in 2 tbsp chopped good-quality black olives. Try with meaty fish, chicken, and lamb.

basil and tomato butter
Pound 6 tbsp salted butter with about 24 torn basil leaves, 2 tbsp coarsely chopped oil-packed sun-dried tomatoes, 1 crushed garlic clove, and freshly ground pepper. Works well with both chicken and fish.

chile and cilantro butter
Pound 6 tbsp salted butter with about 4 heaping tbsp finely chopped fresh cilantro, 1 crushed garlic clove, the grated zest and juice of ½ lime, salt, and pepper. Mix in 1 medium fresh red chile, halved, seeded, and finely chopped. Works brilliantly with nearly everything, including hot corn on the cob.

pasta

Pasta is convenient. Nests of dried tagliatelle can sit happily in the cupboard for years. Pasta is quick to cook and, since you only need a fork, it can be eaten in front of the television, on the floor, or in bed. But it has to be prepared with care.

This is my standby pasta dish. I always have the ingredients for it and I often prefer it to something more complicated. Its simplicity is very satisfying.

· · · · · ·

spaghetti with parsley, red pepper, and garlic

serves 4

8 oz spaghetti

3 tbsp extra virgin olive oil

2 cloves garlic, sliced

1 tsp dried red pepper flakes

salt and pepper

juice of ½ lemon

a generous handful of fresh flat-leaf parsley, finely chopped

I Cook the pasta in plenty of boiling salted water until al dente. While it's cooking, heat the oil in a large frying pan and sauté the garlic and pepper flakes for 1 to 1½ minutes. The garlic should be pale gold. Drain the pasta and immediately add to the frying pan. Season with salt and pepper, add the lemon juice and parsley, and heat for about 30 seconds.

and also...

spaghetti with anchovies, parsley, and vermouth
Cook ½ chopped onion and 3 sliced garlic cloves in 4 tbsp olive oil until soft. Add 2 (2-oz) cans anchovies (drained). Press the anchovies with a wooden spoon to help them disintegrate, then turn up the heat, and add 2 tbsp vermouth, pepper, a handful of chopped parsley, some lemon, and a slug of extra virgin olive oil and toss with cooked, drained spaghetti.

Somehow, although this dish takes no more effort than bacon and eggs, it elevates those very ordinary ingredients.

. . . . . .

spaghetti with bacon, egg, and smoked cheese

serves 2

6 oz spaghetti

3 tbsp olive oil

4 oz bacon

2 large eggs

salt and pepper

2 tbsp extra virgin olive oil

1 tbsp coarsely chopped fresh flat-leaf parsley

2 oz smoked cheese, grated

I Cook the spaghetti in plenty of boiling salted water until al dente. When it's almost ready, heat 1 tbsp of the olive oil in a large frying pan and cook the bacon until crisp and well colored. Transfer it into a bowl and heat the rest of the oil. Fry the eggs, spooning the warm oil up over the top of the eggs to cook the yolks. Season with salt and pepper.

2 Drain the pasta, then put it back in the saucepan. Add the extra virgin olive oil, a little salt, pepper, the bacon, and parsley and toss. Divide between two plates, sprinkle on the grated cheese, and top each serving with a fried egg. Serve immediately.

The combination of sweet onions, blue cheese, and walnuts is irresistible.

. . . . . .

penne with roasted onions, gorgonzola, and walnuts

serves 4

3 large onions, halved

6 tbsp olive oil

2 tbsp balsamic vinegar

salt and pepper

12 oz penne or other short, tubular pasta

4 oz Gorgonzola cheese, crumbled

3 tbsp coarsely chopped fresh flat-leaf parsley

⅔ cup toasted walnut pieces

5 tbsp extra virgin olive oil

I Preheat the oven to 375°F. Cut each onion half into crescent-shaped slices, about ⅝ inch thick. Toss in a roasting pan with the olive oil, vinegar, salt, and pepper. Roast for 30 to 35 minutes, shaking the pan every so often. The onions should be tender and slightly charred.

2 Cook the pasta, drain, and return it to the saucepan. Add the onions, cheese, parsley, walnuts, and extra virgin olive oil. Stir and serve.

Good in autumn and winter when basil and pine nuts seem too summery. You can toss torn arugula or baby spinach leaves with the hot pasta before adding the sauce if you want a more substantial dish (or you're trying to boost your intake of greens).

· · · · · ·

pappardelle with ligurian walnut sauce

Like everyone, I turn to pasta when there isn't much food in the house. "What about pasta?" I murmur indifferently. Then I'll feel a little rise of pleasure as I spot some parsley, which can be tossed with spaghetti, extra virgin olive oil, and red pepper flakes, or dried wild mushrooms, which can be soaked and cooked with cream to dress broad strands of tagliatelle.

serves 4

ligurian walnut sauce

1 slice coarse-textured bread

¾ cup shelled walnuts

1 clove garlic

⅓ cup olive oil

½ cup heavy cream

2 oz Parmesan cheese, freshly grated

salt and pepper

12 oz pappardelle

a bunch of fresh flat-leaf parsley (about ⅜ cup), coarsely chopped

I Soak the bread in a little water for 10 minutes or so, then squeeze out the excess. Put this into a mortar or a food processor with the walnuts and garlic and pound or blend. Stir in the olive oil, cream, Parmesan, salt, and pepper. You should have a thick, creamy sauce.

2 Cook the pappardelle in plenty of boiling salted water until al dente. Mix 2 tbsp of the pasta-cooking water with the sauce, then drain the pasta. Toss the pasta with the sauce and the parsley and serve immediately.

Black pasta looks sensational — very dramatic — so it's good to have a package in the cupboard. You can make this with large shrimp instead of squid and use dried red pepper flakes if you don't have a fresh chile.

. . . . . .

black pasta with squid, chile, and garlic

serves 2

6 oz black pasta, either spaghetti or linguine

1 lb squid, cleaned and prepared

¼ cup olive oil

6 cloves garlic, sliced

1 fresh red chile, halved, seeded, and finely shredded

1 tbsp chopped fresh flat-leaf parsley

juice of ½ lemon

salt and pepper

¼ cup extra virgin olive oil

I Cook the pasta in plenty of boiling salted water until al dente. While it's cooking, wash the squid, making sure to remove any gunk from inside the bodies, and pat dry. Cut the wings from the main bodies. If the squid are large, slice these wings into three or four strips, then cut the body in half lengthwise, and cut the halves into strips about ½ inch wide. If the squid are small, you need only cut off the little wings and then slice the whole body into rings, again about ½ inch wide.

2 When the pasta is almost ready, heat the olive oil in a large frying pan or wok — the oil must get really hot. Stir-fry the squid for about 40 seconds, then turn the heat down a little, and add the garlic and chile. Cook for another 30 seconds or so. (The garlic should turn pale golden; be careful not to burn it.) Throw in the parsley, squeeze on the lemon, and season with salt and pepper. Quickly drain the pasta and toss it with the extra virgin olive oil and the squid. Serve immediately.

Warm pasta, soft ricotta salata, and sweet vegetables make a wonderful interplay of textures and temperatures. Look for trofie online or at specialty food stores.

· · · · · ·

trofie with bacon, peas, ricotta, and mint

serves 4

12 oz trofie or other short pasta

8 oz bacon

¼ cup olive oil

2 cups frozen petite peas

salt and pepper

⅜ cup fresh mint leaves, torn

8 oz ricotta salata cheese (fresh if possible), coarsely broken up

¼ cup extra virgin olive oil

freshly grated Parmesan cheese, for serving

I Cook the pasta in plenty of boiling salted water until al dente. While the pasta is cooking, fry the bacon in the olive oil until it is cooked and golden on all sides. Add the peas and about ¼ cup water and cook until the peas are tender and the water has disappeared. Season with salt and pepper.

2 Drain the pasta and toss it with the bacon, peas, and mint. Gently mix in the ricotta, drizzle with the extra virgin olive oil, season again, and serve with freshly grated Parmesan.

Shrimp and feta might seem like strange bedfellows, but they work very well (as Greeks know). This is a really bright, summery dish.

· · · · · ·

trofie with shrimp, feta, parsley, and lemon

serves 4

12 oz trofie or other short pasta

2 lbs raw shelled shrimp

4 tbsp olive oil

3 cloves garlic, finely chopped

finely grated zest of 1 lemon

juice of ½ lemon

pepper

6 oz feta cheese, crumbled

¼ cup coarsely chopped fresh flat-leaf parsley

¼ cup extra virgin olive oil

I Cook the pasta in plenty of boiling salted water until al dente. While it's cooking, sauté the shrimp for about 2 minutes in the olive oil. Add the garlic and cook for another minute. Throw in the lemon zest and juice and some pepper.

2 Drain the pasta, return it to the pan, and gently mix in the shrimp, feta, parsley, and extra virgin olive oil. Serve immediately.

You can use store-bought stock for this, but add some dry Marsala or white wine if you do, because commercial stock tends to have a less rich flavor than homemade.

· · · · · ·

tagliatelle with wild mushroom sauce

serves 4

½ oz dried wild mushrooms

1 tbsp salted butter

3 oz cultivated mushrooms, cleaned and roughly chopped

1½ cups well-flavored chicken stock

½ cup heavy cream

salt and pepper

1 lb tagliatelle

freshly grated Parmesan cheese, for serving

I Pour boiling water over the dried mushrooms and leave to soak for 15 minutes. Melt the butter and sauté the other mushrooms until well colored. Drain the wild mushrooms, reserving the soaking liquid. Add the mushrooms to the pan and cook for a minute. Pour on the chicken stock and the soaking liquid and cook until the liquid is reduced by two-thirds. Add the cream and simmer until the sauce coats the back of a spoon. Taste and season with salt and pepper.

2 Cook the pasta in boiling salted water, drain, and dress with the sauce. Serve with grated Parmesan.

Simple but somehow luxurious — I think it's the abundance of lemon. You can use flakes of cooked salmon instead of prosciutto, and add asparagus when it's in season.

· · · · · ·

tagliatelle with lemon, peas, and prosciutto

serves 4

1 cup heavy cream

finely grated zest of 4 lemons

juice of 1½ lemons

12 oz tagliatelle

8 oz frozen petite peas or fresh baby peas

2 oz Parmesan cheese, grated, plus more for serving

salt and pepper

6 oz prosciutto, torn into strips about ⅝ inch wide

a small bunch of chervil, coarsely chopped

I Put the cream and the lemon zest and juice into a sauté pan and bring to a boil. Reduce by a third (be careful: it reduces very quickly). Cook the tagliatelle in plenty of boiling salted water until al dente, and cook the peas until just tender.

2 Add the peas, Parmesan, and salt and pepper to the cream. Drain the pasta and add it to the pan along with the prosciutto and the chervil. Heat everything through gently for about 20 seconds and serve immediately with extra grated Parmesan.

serves 4

12 oz tagliatelle

12 oz hot-smoked salmon

1 tbsp unsalted butter

¼ cup vodka or dry white wine

1¼ cups sour cream

¼ cup chopped fresh dill

freshly ground black pepper

4 heaping tsp salmon or red caviar

Good for a midweek supper with friends. The salmon caviar makes it special, but you can leave it out (it's expensive). Add cooked peas or little spears of asparagus when they're in season. You can use smoked trout instead of salmon, or a mixture of smoked and fresh cooked salmon.

· · · · · ·

I Cook the tagliatelle in plenty of boiling salted water until al dente. While it's cooking, break the hot-smoked salmon into flakes, discarding the skin. Melt the butter in a frying pan and add the salmon. Cook for about a minute, then add the vodka. Continue to cook until most of the alcohol has evaporated. Add the sour cream and heat through, but don't allow it to boil. Add the dill and pepper (you shouldn't need salt because the salmon and the caviar are salty).

2 Drain the pasta and add it to the sauce in the pan. Toss everything together, then divide among four warm plates or bowls. Put a spoonful of caviar on the top of each serving.

tagliatelle with hot-smoked salmon, sour cream, and vodka

I find basil pesto just a little cloying, so I like the tartness goat cheese brings. It might seem like a strange combination, but this is also good with sautéed strips of bitter radicchio instead of tomatoes.

· · · · · ·

fettuccine with goat cheese pesto and roasted tomatoes

serves 4

24 cherry tomatoes (about 1 lb)

2 tbsp olive oil

salt and pepper

12 oz fettuccine

goat cheese pesto

3 oz (about 1 cup) basil leaves

3 tbsp pine nuts

2 cloves garlic

⅓ cup freshly grated Parmesan cheese

salt and pepper

¾ cup extra virgin olive oil

4 oz soft goat cheese

I Preheat the oven to 375°F. Put the tomatoes in a roasting pan, drizzle with the olive oil, and season with salt and pepper. Roast for 20 to 25 minutes, until they are completely soft and a little charred. They can be either hot or at room temperature when added to the pasta.

2 Cook the fettuccine in plenty of boiling salted water until al dente.

3 Put the basil, pine nuts, garlic, half the Parmesan, and salt and pepper into a food processor. Blend, gradually adding the extra virgin olive oil, then stir in the rest of the Parmesan. Break up the goat cheese and gently stir it into the pesto. Check the seasoning.

4 Drain the pasta and toss in a warmed bowl with the pesto and the roasted tomatoes.

greens
and
herbs
• • • • • •

Georgian cooking is full of walnuts, pomegranates, and cilantro. They're wonderful in combination and very pretty to look at.

· · · · · ·

georgian eggplant salad with walnuts, pomegranates, and cilantro

serves 4

3 eggplants

olive oil

salt and pepper

1 cup Greek-style yogurt

½ cup walnut pieces, toasted

3 oz (about 1 cup) fresh cilantro leaves

seeds from 1 pomegranate

dressing

1½ tbsp pomegranate molasses

2 cloves garlic, crushed

1 medium fresh red chile, halved, seeded, and very thinly sliced

1 tsp honey, or to taste

a really good squeeze of lemon juice

salt and pepper

5 tbsp extra virgin olive oil

I Preheat the oven to 400°F. Trim the ends off the eggplants and cut them lengthwise into slices about ⅜ inch thick. Toss the slices in a bowl (you can do this in batches) with olive oil, salt, and pepper. Be generous: the slices should be well coated. Put them on baking sheets and roast for about 25 minutes. The eggplant should be golden and soft. (You can fry the eggplant if you prefer.)

2 To make the dressing, mix together the molasses, garlic, chile, honey, lemon juice, salt, and pepper. Whisk in the olive oil. Taste for seasoning. Eggplant is quite bland, so it can take a strongly flavored dressing.

3 Pour two-thirds of the dressing over the warm eggplant and leave them to soak it up if you have time.

4 To assemble the salad, layer the eggplant in a broad shallow bowl with the yogurt, walnuts, cilantro, salt, and pepper. Sprinkle the pomegranate seeds over the top and drizzle with the rest of the dressing.

greens and herbs

serves 4 as a main course

1 (2¼-lb) butternut squash

3 tbsp olive oil

salt and pepper

1 tsp superfine sugar

1 fresh red chile, halved, seeded,
and finely shredded

6 oz (about 2¼ cups) salad greens (I like a
mixture of baby spinach and watercress)

6 oz feta cheese, broken into chunks

¼ cup pitted black olives

dressing

1½ tsp white wine vinegar

a smidgen of Dijon mustard

salt and pepper

5 tbsp extra virgin olive oil

a generous pinch of superfine sugar

Roasted squash is great in winter salads; it's a meaty ingredient with a wonderful color. It's also much less hassle to prepare than you might expect: you don't even have to peel the slices because the skin becomes so soft during roasting. This dish is a nice mixture of sweet and salty flavors.

• • • • • •

roasted squash, feta, and black olive salad

I Preheat the oven to 400°F. Halve the squash and remove the seeds. Cut into slices lengthwise (about ⅝ inch wide at the thickest part) and put on a baking tray. Drizzle with the olive oil, and sprinkle with salt, pepper, and the sugar. Turn over with your hands, making sure the squash gets well coated. Roast for 25 minutes. Sprinkle the chile over the squash in the last 10 minutes of roasting time. Leave the squash to cool a little.

2 Make the dressing by putting the vinegar, mustard, and some salt and pepper into a cup, then whisking in the extra virgin olive oil with a fork. Add a little sugar, then taste and adjust the seasoning.

3 Toss the greens with two-thirds of the dressing in a broad, shallow bowl. Put the squash, feta, and olives on top. Drizzle on the remaining dressing.

Figs are luxurious and sexy, so perfect for making a salad seem special. You could use a blue cheese instcad of the goat cheese, or substitute smoked duck or warm duck breast for the cheese.

. . . . . .

goat cheese and fig salad

serves 4

dressing

a smidgen of Dijon mustard

salt and pepper

1½ tbsp red wine vinegar

1 tsp crème de cassis (black currant liqueur)

2 tbsp olive oil and 6 tbsp hazelnut oil

12 figs, halved, brushed with olive oil, and sprinkled with a little superfine sugar

8 oz (about 3 cups) salad greens: baby spinach, watercress, or lamb's lettuce (mâche), or a mixture

½ cup shelled hazelnuts, halved and toasted

8 oz goat cheese, broken into chunks

I For the dressing, shake all the ingredients together in a jar. Check the seasoning.

2 Heat a ridged grill pan over medium heat and cook the figs, cut-side down, for about 3 minutes, until soft and caramelized.

3 Toss the greens and nuts with most of the dressing, then arrange the figs and cheese on top. Drizzle with the rest of the dressing and serve.

This recipe is adapted from one in a book called *Verdura* by Viana La Place, which makes me want to eat vegetables all the time. Who can resist a dish with such a name?

. . . . . .

dama bianca

serves 4

1 lb fresh mozzarella cheese

2 fennel bulbs

2 pale green celery stalks, plus any leaves attached

salt and pepper

juice of 1 lemon

½ cup extra virgin olive oil

shavings of Parmesan or pecorino cheese (optional)

I Drain the mozzarella and dry with paper towels.

2 Cut off any feathery bits on the fennel and save them. Halve each bulb and trim the bottom. Slice each half thinly with a sharp knife, or a mandoline if you have one. Trim the celery stalks and cut into fine (julienne) strips. Tear the celery leaves very coarsely.

3 Cut the mozzarella into thin slices and arrange on a platter or individual plates, alternating them with the fennel, celery, and celery leaves. Season with salt, pepper, and lemon juice as you go, and drizzle with some of the olive oil. Snip any feathery bits of fennel over the top. Sprinkle on the Parmesan and finish with a drizzle of olive oil.

Always on the menu in a raffish Parisian bistro called Le Petit Gavroche, this is one of my favorite salads.

. . . . . .

salade gavrocharde

serves 4

dressing

1 tsp white wine vinegar

a smidgen of Dijon mustard

salt and pepper

a pinch of superfine sugar

¼ cup extra virgin olive oil

4 oz (about 1½ cups) salad greens
(I like frisée and baby spinach)

12 full-flavored tomatoes, quartered

½ cup walnut pieces, toasted

4 oz Roquefort cheese, crumbled

I Make the dressing by whisking all the ingredients together with a fork. Toss the salad ingredients with the dressing and serve immediately.

and also...

salade de nevers
Make the salad as above, adding 6 oz bacon, cooked until crisp, and topping each serving with a poached egg.

A French bistro classic. The walnuts can be replaced with hazelnuts and the Roquefort with Gorgonzola or another blue cheese.

. . . . . .

pear, roquefort, and walnut salad

serves 2

dressing

1¼ tsp white wine vinegar

½ tsp Dijon mustard

salt and pepper

½ tsp superfine sugar, or to taste

2 tbsp walnut oil

1½ tbsp light olive oil

2 small ripe pears, halved and cored

lemon juice, if necessary

½ cup walnut halves

4 oz (about 1½ cups) salad greens (a mixture of watercress and Belgian endive)

4 oz Roquefort cheese, crumbled

I Make the dressing by mixing together the vinegar, mustard, salt, pepper, and sugar. Slowly whisk in the oils and then check the seasoning.

2 Cut the pears into slices lengthwise. If you are not serving immediately, squeeze fresh lemon juice over them to prevent browning. Just before serving, toss all the ingredients together with the dressing.

In ceviche, a specialty of South America, the lime juice "cooks" the raw fish. Healthy as well as delicious.

· · · · · ·

salmon ceviche with avocado and mango

serves 4 as a main course

1 (¾-lb) salmon fillet, skin removed

juice of 2 limes

2 medium fresh red chiles, seeded and cut into slivers

2 scallions, thinly sliced

salt and pepper

1 mango (not so ripe that it's soft)

2 avocados

1 cup firmly packed fresh cilantro leaves and stems

½ cup fresh mint leaves

dressing

juice of 1 lime

5 tbsp olive oil

salt and pepper

1 tsp superfine sugar, or to taste

I Cut the salmon into paper-thin slices. Lay on a large plate or tray and squeeze the lime juice over the top. Sprinkle on the chiles and scallions, and season well with salt and pepper. Turn the pieces over so that everything gets coated and leave for 5 minutes.

2 Make the dressing by mixing the lime juice with the olive oil, some salt and pepper, and the sugar. Taste to check whether you need to make any adjustments.

3 Peel the mango and cut off the "cheeks" (the fleshy parts on either side of the pit). Cut these cheeks into slices about ⅛ inch thick. (Use the rest of the mango flesh for something else; it is difficult to remove it and keep it firm and intact.) Halve the avocados and remove the pits. Cut each half into slices, then peel the skin from each slice. Work carefully to avoid squashing the flesh. Gently toss the mango and avocado with the salmon, dressing, cilantro, and mint. Serve at once.

Scandinavian-inspired. The cold acidity of the buttermilk really cuts through the richness of the bacon and fish. You can use smoked trout or fresh salmon instead of hot-smoked salmon, and can include quarters of cooked beets as well (but not pickled beets).

· · · · · ·

hot-smoked salmon, bacon, and potato salad with buttermilk dressing

serves 4 as a main course

dressing

1⅓ cups buttermilk

6 tbsp heavy cream

1 clove garlic, finely chopped

2 tbsp finely chopped fresh dill

black pepper

1 lb small waxy potatoes

1 tbsp salted butter

8 oz green beans, trimmed

8 oz pancetta or bacon

12 oz hot-smoked salmon

12 oz (about 4 cups) watercress

I To make the dressing, mix everything together and put it in the refrigerator until you need it.

2 Try to cook everything (except the hot-smoked salmon, of course) at the last minute so that you have a salad that contains different temperatures. Boil the potatoes until tender, drain, and toss in the butter. Cover. Boil the beans until al dente. Fry the pancetta in its own fat until cooked and colored on all sides.

3 Break up the salmon into very large flakes, discarding the skin. Gently toss the potatoes, watercress, and beans with most of the buttermilk dressing, put the salmon and pancetta on top, and drizzle over the rest of the dressing.

and also...

smoked mackerel, potato, and beet salad

Make the salad as above, but use smoked mackerel instead of salmon (again, remove the skin), omit the pancetta, and use 8 oz cooked beets. Halve or quarter the globes of beets and quickly sauté them in a little butter until they are warm. Arrange them with the rest of the salad at the last minute (otherwise the color from the beets will stain the other ingredients) and dress.

Preserved or pickled lemons are now available in many supermarkets and specialty food stores. You can serve this salad at room temperature rather than warm (which makes it a great lunch), but don't add the herbs until just before serving.

. . . . . .

warm chicken, roasted pepper, chickpea, and preserved lemon salad

serves 4 as a main course

3 red bell peppers, halved, with stems and seeds removed

olive oil

salt and pepper

4 skinless chicken breast fillets

1 (14-oz) can chickpeas, drained and rinsed

1 preserved lemon, flesh discarded and rind cut into slivers

a good handful of fresh flat-leaf parsley or cilantro leaves (about ⅜ cup), very coarsely chopped

dressing

3 cloves garlic

3½ tbsp pine nuts

6 tbsp extra virgin olive oil

juice of ½ lemon

salt and pepper

I Preheat the oven to 375°F. Lay the peppers in a roasting pan. Drizzle over about 5 tbsp olive oil and season with salt and pepper. Roast for about 35 minutes, or until the peppers are soft and slightly charred.

2 For the dressing, put the garlic and pine nuts into a food processor and, with the motor running, pour in the oil. Add the lemon juice and season to taste.

3 When the peppers are cooked, cut them into wide strips. You can remove the skin first but I hardly ever do.

4 Brush the chicken with oil and season with salt and pepper. Heat a ridged grill pan over medium-high heat and cook the breasts for about 2 minutes on each side; don't try to turn them before, or you could tear the flesh. (Or you can simply fry the breasts in a frying pan.) Lower the heat and cook for another 2½ to 3 minutes on each side, or until the chicken is cooked through.

5 Slice the chicken and toss with the roasted peppers, chickpeas, preserved lemon, herbs, and dressing. Serve immediately.

An utterly beautiful-looking winter salad. Who says cold-weather food has to be brown? I sometimes add torn mozzarella, crumbled goat cheese, or Gorgonzola as well.

. . . . . .

pear, fig, and prosciutto salad with pomegranates

serves 4

½ pomegranate

2 heads Belgian endive

2 heads radicchio

4 small pears

juice of 1 lemon

6 ripe figs, quartered

6 tbsp extra virgin olive oil

salt and pepper

12 slices prosciutto

I To remove the seeds from the pomegranate, hold the half fruit over a bowl and beat hard with a wooden spoon; the seeds should tumble out. If they don't (your pomegranate may not be ripe enough), then gouge out the seeds with a spoon and remove the creamy, bitter pith attached to them. Pull the leaves of the endive and radicchio apart.

2 Halve and core the pears and cut into slices about ¼ inch wide. Immediately put them into half the lemon juice and turn them over in it — this stops the flesh from turning brown.

3 Arrange the endive, radicchio, pear slices, and fig quarters on a platter. Drizzle with some extra virgin olive oil and pour the rest of the lemon juice over the top. Season with salt and pepper. Tear the prosciutto into wide strips and lay these over the fruit and leaves. Sprinkle on the pomegranate seeds. Drizzle again with a little extra virgin olive oil and sprinkle with some freshly ground black pepper. Serve immediately.

If you can't find Cashel Blue —
a gorgeous Irish cheese that I always
think tastes faintly of smoked bacon —
then use Gorgonzola instead.

· · · · · ·

salad of seared beef and cashel blue cheese

serves 4 as a starter

dressing

2¼ tsp white wine vinegar

a smidgen of Dijon mustard

a pinch of superfine sugar

6 tbsp extra virgin olive oil

1 (12-oz) piece of beef tenderloin, trimmed

salt and pepper

2 tbsp peanut oil

3 oz (about 1 cup) sharp-tasting greens (such as arugula and watercress)

½ red onion, very finely sliced

4 oz Cashel Blue cheese, crumbled

I Make the dressing by whisking all the ingredients together with a fork.

2 Sprinkle the beef with salt and pepper. Heat the oil in a frying pan until very hot, then cook the beef for about 2 minutes on each side — the beef should remain totally rare inside. Leave the meat to rest a little.

3 Mix the salad greens in a bowl with the onion and cheese and most of the dressing. Toss and divide among four plates. Slice the beef and lay it on top of the salads. Grind some pepper over the top and drizzle on the rest of the dressing.

The starter is my favorite part of any meal. It's small, designed to stimulate rather than sate the appetite, and can be just an assembly of good ingredients. For suppers with friends — especially midweek — or when you want to spoil yourself a bit, try the following. Evidence that simple can be very chic.

......

(virtually) no-cook starters

radishes, sweet butter, and sea salt

One of the chicest starters imaginable. Get really fresh French breakfast radishes (the leaves should be sprightly, not droopy) and wash well. Serve with really good unsalted butter and a baguette or sourdough bread. The idea is to spread the peppery radishes with the butter and eat them with sea salt and bread. Wrinkled black olives and rounds of salami are good along with this.

claqueret

One of those dishes you find in provincial French cheese shops or old-fashioned French homes. It's a light, slightly tangy dip, which you can spread on toasted croûtes (crostini) or serve with radishes. Simply mash together 12 oz mild goat cheese, 6 tbsp crème fraîche, 1 tbsp each of white wine vinegar and dry white wine, 2 tbsp extra virgin olive oil, 2 crushed garlic cloves, 2 tbsp each of chopped parsley and chives, and a good grinding of black pepper. Cover and refrigerate until you need it. It's best made the day before.

quail eggs with dukkah

A North African street snack, and a classy opener to a meal. To make the dukkah, toast ½ cup blanched hazelnuts in a dry frying pan, then toast 7 tbsp sesame seeds with 3 tbsp each of cumin and coriander seeds. Let everything cool, then either pound the nuts and spices with a mortar and pestle, or pulse-blend them in a food processor (you want to end up with a powdery mixture, with coarse bits throughout, not a paste, so be careful if you are using a food processor). Cook the quail eggs in a pan of boiling water for 4 minutes and serve with sea salt and a bowl of dukkah.

eggs with mayo

Yes, hard-boiled eggs can be smart. Be sure to use a good store-bought mayo. Mix it with a couple of tbsp of fromage blanc or crème fraîche and a good squeeze of lemon juice, and flavor with chopped black olives and anchovies; or shredded sorrel or other herbs, such as chervil, basil, or parsley; or finely chopped red onion and capers. Serve with hard-boiled hen eggs or quail eggs. Quail eggs take just 4 minutes to hard-boil.

spanish tapas

Tapas doesn't have to mean making tortillas or frying shrimp. Just serve good, coarse country bread with rounds of chorizo; cured anchovies in olive oil (go for a really good brand such as Ortiz); manchego cheese and the quince jelly called membrillo (now available in many specialty food stores); and Serrano ham or jamón iberico (the latter is an expensive but delicious cured ham, from pigs fed on acorns), with capers, salted almonds, and green olives.

little potatoes with crème fraîche and caviar

This became almost a cliché (totally passé as a smart canapé) but, as with many things that get labeled as "so over," it is delicious and beautifully simple. Cook small new potatoes until tender, then serve them with a small bowl of red salmon caviar and another bowl of crème fraîche and let guests help themselves.

asparagus

Still such a fleeting seasonal pleasure that it doesn't require much adornment. Serve steamed with melted salted butter. Or drizzle with extra virgin olive oil, a touch of balsamic vinegar, and shower with shavings of Parmesan.

prosciutto and fruit

Cured ham with fruit may take you back to the Italian trattoria dishes which were edged out by more fashionable Italian peasant food, but it's still a great combination. Serve fatty pink slices with fresh figs, sliced ripe pears (prepare just before serving and squeeze a little lemon juice on the slices to keep them from turning brown), or peeled wedges of mango.

fava beans, ham, and pecorino

This makes a lovely starter when the beans first come into season in May, when they are small and sweet enough to eat raw. Just remove the beans from the pod and toss them with shavings of pecorino cheese, slivers of prosciutto, black pepper, and extra virgin olive oil. You can blanch the beans if you prefer, then slip off their little thin skins, to reveal a wonderful, bright greenness, before combining with the other ingredients.

vegetables in pinzimonio

Simple and very summery. Provide each diner with a little glass or bowl full of really good extra virgin olive oil (about ¼ cup per person; it is worth splashing out on a delicious single-estate oil). Have sea salt and black pepper available. Serve with a platter of perfect raw vegetables, or a mixture of raw and blanched vegetables. Cherry tomatoes, thin slices of fennel, florets of cauliflower, young carrots, blanched green beans, steamed asparagus, cooked artichoke heart — whatever is good and in season.

vegetables with bagna cauda

A Piedmontese dish, though there's also a Provençal version. Serve perfect raw or cooked vegetables (or a mixture of raw and cooked — I often include strips of roasted pepper) with an anchovy dipping sauce. Gently heat 1 cup olive oil with 3 tbsp salted butter and add 2 garlic cloves, peeled and very finely chopped. Cook until soft but not colored, then add 10 chopped anchovy fillets and cook until the anchovies have disintegrated. Add pepper. That's it. Ideally this should be kept warm with a little burner underneath it, but it does retain its heat for a while so just serve one bowl or individual little ramekins of it. Hard-boiled hen or quail eggs are good with this too.

rye bread and hot-smoked salmon

A bit different from brown bread and cold-smoked salmon. Butter squares or triangles of rye bread and top with pieces of hot-smoked salmon (remove the skin), a tsp of sour cream, and a sprig of dill.

toast skagen

Swedish and very easy to throw together. Combine 1 lb peeled shrimp with ½ cup sour cream, ½ cup mayonnaise, lemon juice, and plenty of chopped fresh dill and chives. Toast rounds of bread and top with the shrimp mixture and a little red caviar, if you can afford it.

spring and summer veggies

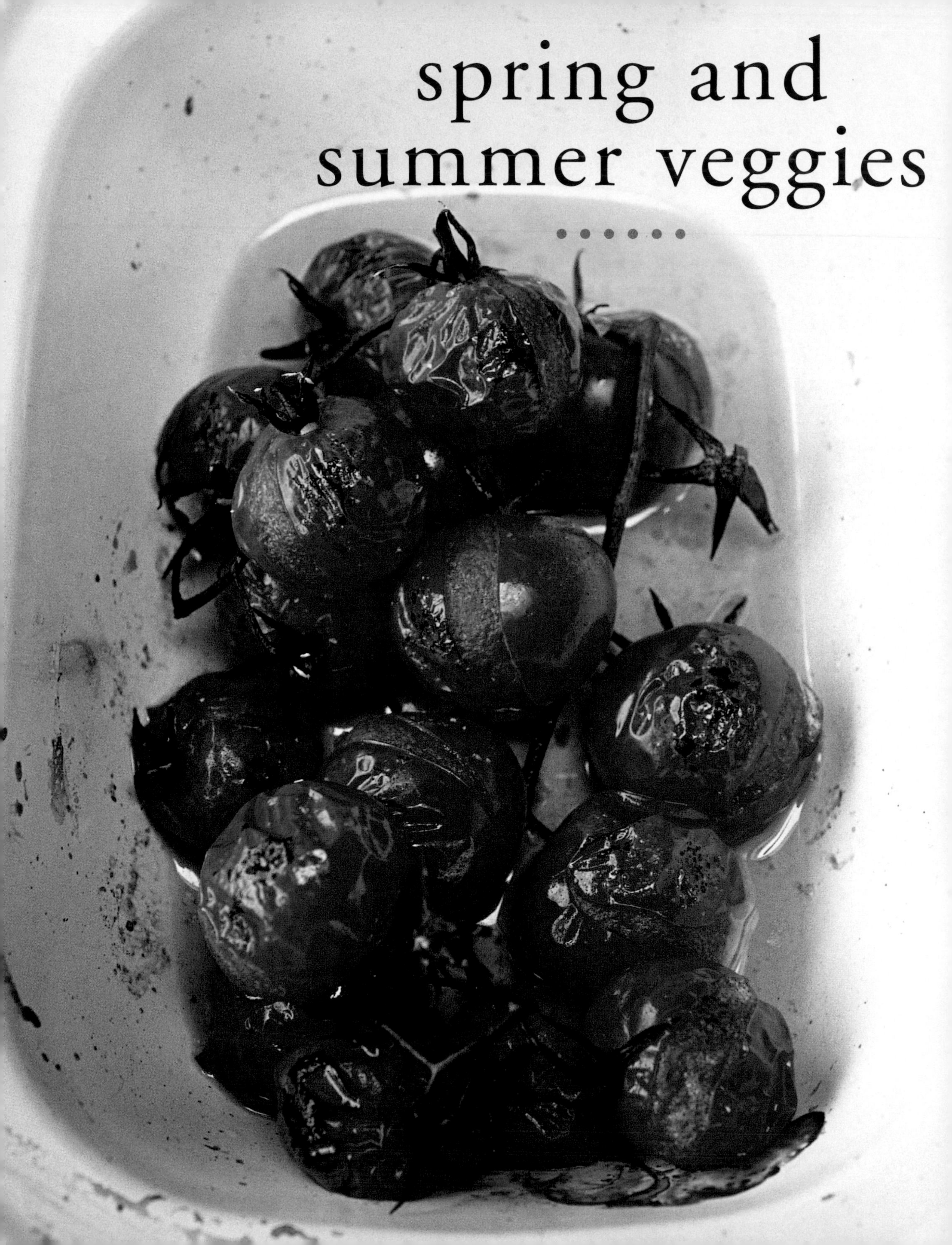

I love eggplant. They look like Ali Baba's slippers and have a velvety flesh that will absorb a whole array of flavors but still taste of itself. I'm not so fond of frying or broiling them because it takes forever, but have found that slices can be roasted successfully as long as they are well coated in oil. And don't get in a tizzy about the amount of oil; it is olive, after all. All of these make good starters or side dishes, or are good as part of a spread of Mediterranean mezze or antipasti.

· · · · · ·

roasted eggplant three ways

serves 4 as a starter or side dish

3 eggplants

olive oil

salt and pepper

lemon juice or balsamic vinegar (optional)

I Preheat the oven to 400°F. Trim the ends off the eggplants and cut them lengthwise into slices about ⅜ inch thick. Toss the slices in a bowl with olive oil, salt, and pepper. Make sure the oil is rubbed in. Put them on baking sheets and roast for about 25 minutes. The eggplants should be golden and soft. If they're at all dry, leave them to marinate in lemon juice (or a little balsamic vinegar) and extra virgin olive oil. Try serving them . . .

with pecorino and chile
Halve 2 fresh red chiles, seed, and cut into thin strips. Gently sauté with 4 thinly sliced garlic cloves until pale gold and sprinkle over the eggplant. Squeeze the juice of ½ lemon on top, season with salt and pepper, shower with shavings of pecorino (use a potato peeler), and drizzle with extra virgin olive oil.

with hummus, yogurt, mint, and cilantro
Puree 1 (14-oz) can of drained chickpeas, ⅔ cup extra virgin olive oil, the juice of 1 lemon, 1 garlic clove, 1½ tbsp tahini, 1 heaping tsp cayenne pepper, and 1 tsp ground cumin in a food processor. Season with salt and pepper. Tear mint and cilantro leaves over the eggplant slices and serve with the hummus, with plain Greek-style yogurt spooned alongside.

with salsa verde
Into a food processor put 8 anchovy fillets, 10 basil leaves, 15 mint leaves, leaves from a small bunch of flat-leaf parsley, 1½ tsp Dijon mustard, 1 garlic clove, and 1 tbsp capers, rinsed of salt or brine. Pulse, adding ⅔ cup extra virgin olive oil. Taste and add lemon juice. Serve spooned over the eggplant slices.

serves 4 as a starter or side dish

4 eggplants

olive oil

salt and pepper

2 onions, thinly sliced

6 cloves garlic, thinly sliced

2 medium fresh red chiles, halved, seeded, and thinly sliced

juice of ½ lemon

4 oz feta cheese, crumbled

¾ cup Greek-style yogurt

a handful of fresh mint leaves, torn

extra virgin olive oil

I've never eaten this in Turkey. Somebody described it to me, and I came up with this dish — so I can't claim it as authentic but who cares? It is a lip-smacking combination of textures and temperatures. Substantial enough to be a main course if you want to serve it that way.

· · · · · ·

turkish baked eggplant with chile, feta, and mint

I Preheat the oven to 400°F. Halve the eggplants lengthwise and then score a diamond pattern into the flesh of each half on the cut surface, being careful not to cut all the way through. Pour about 10 tbsp olive oil over them and season with salt and pepper. Turn them over to make sure they are well coated. Roast for 40 to 45 minutes.

2 While the eggplants are cooking, sauté the onions in ¼ cup olive oil until soft and golden. Add the garlic and chiles and cook for another 2 minutes, until they are soft as well.

3 When the eggplants are tender put them on a serving plate, cut-side up, and squeeze lemon juice over them. Gently press the cooked flesh down to make a bit of room for the onions. Fill the eggplant cavities with the onion and sprinkle the feta on top.

4 Daub the yogurt over the eggplants and throw on the mint leaves. Drizzle extra virgin olive oil over the top before serving. You can serve this warm or at room temperature.

Summer arrives and you can find yourself serving nothing but bowls of gluey potato salad. But dress potatoes while they're still hot, leave them so that the waxy flesh can soak up the flavors, and you have quite a different dish. You can eat this warm or at room temperature, and make it well ahead of when you want to serve it. Use small new potatoes for these recipes.

· · · · · ·

warm potatoes and beans with avocado

and also...

warm potatoes and beans with pesto

Prepare the potatoes and beans as below, using 1 lb potatoes and 6 oz green beans. While they are cooking, make some pesto by pureeing ½ cup freshly grated Parmesan, 1 garlic clove, ¼ cup pine nuts, 2 oz basil leaves, and 6 tbsp extra virgin olive oil in a food processor. Taste and season. Toss the cooked vegetables with a couple of tbsp extra virgin olive oil and season. Add a little of the bean cooking water to the pesto to loosen it, then toss the pesto with the vegetables. Great with lamb.

potatoes with shallots and capers

Cook 1¼ lbs potatoes as in the main recipe. Slice 4 shallots and cook them in 1 tbsp olive oil until they are soft but not browned. Put these in a serving bowl with 1½ tbsp rinsed capers and about 1 tbsp chopped fresh flat-leaf parsley. As soon as the potatoes are tender, drain them and add them to the bowl with 2 tbsp extra virgin olive oil, 1½ tsp white wine vinegar, salt, and pepper. Toss everything gently together and serve hot, warm, or at room temperature. This is especially good with fish.

serves 4 as a side dish

dressing

2¼ tsp white wine vinegar

a drop of Dijon mustard

salt and pepper

a good pinch of superfine sugar

⅓ cup extra virgin olive oil

1 avocado

12 oz small new potatoes

4 oz green beans, topped but not tailed

1 Make the dressing by whisking all the ingredients together with a fork.

2 Halve the avocado and remove the pit. Without peeling the avocado, cut each half lengthwise into slices about ⅜ inch thick at the thickest part. Peel the skin from each slice and place the slices in a shallow serving bowl. Pour the dressing over.

3 Cook the potatoes in boiling salted water for 10 to 15 minutes, depending on how small they are, until just tender. Cook the beans while the potatoes are boiling (the beans should still have a little firmness), then drain and run cold water over them to keep the bright green color. Put the beans in the bowl with the avocado. Slice each potato in half, add to the bowl, and gently toss everything together. Using your hands is the easiest way — you just have to be careful not to break up the avocado. Serve immediately, while the potatoes are still warm.

Potatoes crushed with olive oil are a bit of a cliché of modern restaurant menus, but that doesn't mean they're not good. These are great with grilled or baked fish on top.

. . . . . .

potatoes with olives and lemon

serves 4 as a side dish

1¾ lbs new potatoes

1¼ cups black olives in olive oil, pitted

½ cup extra virgin olive oil, plus extra for drizzling

juice of ½ lemon

finely grated zest of 1 lemon

2 tbsp coarsely chopped fresh flat-leaf parsley

salt and pepper

I Cook the potatoes in boiling salted water until tender. Drain but keep the potatoes in the saucepan so they stay warm. Partly crush the potatoes with a masher or fork — you just want them broken up, not mashed — and stir in the olives, olive oil, lemon juice, lemon zest, and parsley. Season with salt and pepper, drizzle with a little olive oil, and serve.

Kind of Spanish, I suppose (it's that smoked paprika again). Good with roasted or grilled chicken or lamb or highly spiced sausages. Topped with a fried egg, it makes a pretty good supper dish.

. . . . . .

roasted potatoes and tomatoes with spices

serves 6 as a side dish

2¼ lbs waxy potatoes, cut into even-sized pieces

1 lb cherry tomatoes, left whole

1 tbsp coriander seeds

1½ tsp cumin seeds

2 tsp pimenton (smoked Spanish paprika)

6 tbsp olive oil

salt and pepper

¼ cup finely chopped fresh flat-leaf parsley or cilantro leaves

I Preheat the oven to 350°F. Spread out the potatoes and tomatoes in a single layer in a roasting pan.

2 In a small frying pan, dry-roast the coriander and cumin seeds. Crush them in a mortar, and add the pimenton and olive oil. Pour over the vegetables, making sure they all are coated, and season well with salt and pepper. Roast for 40 minutes, shaking the pan a couple of times during cooking. Sprinkle with the parsley and serve at once.

Roasted tomatoes are a cinch, plus roasting is a good way to treat tomatoes that are lacking in flavor because it concentrates the sugar content. Make sure you lay the tomatoes in a single layer so that they really roast and don't just sweat.

• • • • • •

roasted tomatoes with herbs and lemon crumbs

serves 6 as a side dish

12 plum tomatoes

¼ cup olive oil

salt and pepper

a little sugar

⅔ cup fresh white bread crumbs

finely grated zest of ½ lemon

1 tsp finely chopped fresh flat-leaf parsley

1 tsp chopped fresh chives

and also...

roasted tomatoes with goat cheese

Make as below, but instead of sprinkling with bread crumbs, top the tomatoes with 4 oz crumbled goat cheese. Drizzle with a little more olive oil, grind on some black pepper, and roast for another 10 minutes, until the cheese is starting to turn pale gold.

hot and sweet roasted tomatoes

Prepare the tomatoes as below. Mix ¼ cup olive oil, 2 tbsp balsamic vinegar, 1 tsp harissa, and 1 tsp superfine sugar in a cup. Pour this over the tomatoes and roast for 45 minutes at 400°F. The tomatoes should be shrunken and sweet. Serve warm or at room temperature, drizzled with extra virgin olive oil and either daubed with plain yogurt or sprinkled with black olives and torn basil leaves.

baked tomatoes with parmesan

Follow the main roasted tomato recipe. Throw about ½ cup grated Parmesan over the tomato halves about 15 minutes before the end of baking. For a creamy cheese gratin, pour ⅔ cup heavy cream over the tomatoes at the end of the roasting time, sprinkle with the cheese, and roast for another 15 minutes, until the cheese is bubbling and golden.

I Preheat the oven to 375°F. Cut each tomato in half and spread in a single layer in a large gratin dish or roasting pan. Drizzle with about half of the olive oil and season with salt and pepper. Using your hands, mix the tomatoes around so that they are well covered with oil. Turn them all cut-side up. Roast for 40 minutes, sprinkling a little sugar over the top after they have cooked for 20 minutes.

2 Sprinkle on the bread crumbs, lemon zest, and herbs. Drizzle again with olive oil and roast for another 15 minutes, or until the bread crumbs are golden. Serve hot or warm.

A spin on roasted Mediterranean vegetables, and very easy to make. Serve as a main course with flatbread or a bowl of couscous into which you have stirred some chopped parsley and maybe some slivers of preserved lemon. It's also a good side dish with roasted or grilled chicken or lamb.

• • • • • •

hot and sweet roasted mediterranean vegetables with tahini dressing

serves 4 as a main course, 6 as a side dish

3 zucchini

2 eggplants

1 red bell pepper and 1 yellow bell pepper

6 tomatoes

1 red onion

¼ cup olive oil

1 tbsp balsamic vinegar

1 tbsp ground cumin

½ tsp ground cinnamon

2 tsp dark brown sugar

2 tsp harissa or West Indian hot sauce

salt and pepper

⅓ cup raisins

¼ cup pine nuts, toasted

2 tbsp coarsely chopped fresh cilantro leaves

dressing

⅔ cup plain yogurt

⅔ cup tahini

juice of 2 lemons

¼ cup water

¼ cup extra virgin olive oil

4 cloves garlic, crushed

salt and pepper

I Preheat the oven to 375°F. Cut the zucchini and the eggplant into rounds about ½ inch thick. Cut the larger eggplant slices in quarters and halve the rest. Halve and seed the peppers and cut each half into 4 or 5 wide strips lengthwise. Quarter the tomatoes and cut the onion into half-moon slices.

2 Put the vegetables into a large roasting pan in a single layer. Mix the oil, vinegar, cumin, cinnamon, brown sugar, and harissa together. Pour this over the vegetables and season well with salt and pepper. Stir the vegetables around to make sure they are all coated. Roast for 25 minutes.

3 Put the raisins in just-boiled water and leave to soak for 20 minutes, then drain and stir into the vegetables. Roast for another 15 minutes or so, or until the vegetables are tender and slightly charred. Stir in the pine nuts.

4 To make the dressing, beat the yogurt into the tahini with a fork or spoon, then add the lemon juice, water, extra virgin olive oil, and garlic. Taste and season with salt and pepper — it needs quite a lot of salt. You may also want to add a little more water or olive oil to thin the mixture.

5 Put the vegetables on a large platter. Leave at room temperature if you are serving in a couple of hours, or refrigerate and bring back to room temperature before you want to serve them. Drizzle with the dressing, sprinkle the cilantro over the top, and serve.

and also...

roasted mediterranean vegetables with preserved lemons
Roast the vegetables as in the main recipe but omit the sugar, spices, raisins, pine nuts, and cilantro. About 10 minutes before the vegetables are due to be ready, stir in the sliced rind of ¾ preserved lemon. The sweetness of the vegetables and sourness of the lemon are delicious together.

roasted mediterranean vegetables with anchovy pesto
Roast the vegetables as in the main recipe but omit the sugar, spices, raisins, pine nuts, and cilantro. Combine a 2-oz can anchovies with oil, 6 tbsp pine nuts, and 1 garlic clove in a food processor. Turn it on and add ¼ cup extra virgin olive oil in a steady stream. Taste and add as much lemon juice as you think it needs (I generally end up adding a little less than ½ lemon), and season with pepper. Chop a small bunch of flat-leaf parsley and stir in. Serve drizzled over the vegetables. This sauce is also good with roasted red peppers.

roasted mediterranean vegetables with white bean skordalia
Skordalia is a Greek garlic sauce, usually made with potato, nuts, or bread. This is a bean one. It's good as a dip for raw vegetables too, and as an accompaniment to grilled fish or lamb. Be sure to pay attention to the seasoning — you need to be generous. Roast the vegetables as in the main recipe but omit the sugar, spices, raisins, pine nuts, and cilantro. Heat 2 tbsp olive oil in a saucepan and cook ½ chopped onion until soft. Add 5 chopped garlic cloves and cook for another couple of minutes, then puree these with a drained (14-oz) can of cannellini beans, ¼ cup extra virgin olive oil, the juice of ½ lemon, and plenty of salt and pepper. Check seasoning. Serve at room temperature with the roasted vegetables.

This may sound like a simple and not very exciting combination, but I practically live on it in the summer when my small patch of zucchini produces more vegetables than I can cope with. It's also well behaved — you can make it earlier in the day to eat in the evening

• • • • • •

zucchini with ricotta, mint, and basil

serves 4 as a main course, 6 as a side dish

6 medium zucchini

olive oil

salt and pepper

12 oz ricotta salata cheese, fresh if possible, broken into chunks

½ cup pecorino cheese shavings

1 small bunch basil, leaves only

1 small bunch mint, leaves only

juice of 1 lemon

extra virgin olive oil

I Have everything ready and on hand because you will layer the dish as you cook it.

2 Cut the zucchini into rounds about ¼ inch thick. Heat 2 tbsp olive oil in a large pan and cook the zucchini, in batches, until golden on each side and tender. Add more olive oil as you need it and season the zucchini with salt and pepper as you cook them. Put the zucchini in the bottom of a broad shallow bowl and cook the next batch. When you have a layer, put some ricotta, pecorino, and herbs on the top, plus a good squeeze of lemon and a drizzle of extra virgin olive oil. Continue like this until you've layered all the zucchini. Finish with some herbs and shavings of pecorino and drizzle with a bit of extra virgin olive oil. Serve while still warm, or at room temperature.

One of the easiest and best-liked dishes I cook. You can use this stuffing as a kind of blueprint and add a little chopped red chiles and anchovies, or some sautéed spicy sausage and onion.

• • • • • •

sicilian baked stuffed peppers

serves 6 as a starter or a side dish

3 cups fresh white bread crumbs from coarse country bread with good flavor

⅓ cup currants

6 tbsp pine nuts, toasted

¼ cup capers, rinsed of salt or brine

3 tbsp pitted chopped black olives

½ cup combined fresh parsley and mint leaves, coarsely chopped

¼ cup olive oil, plus extra for drizzling

salt and pepper

6 large red bell peppers, halved and seeded

I Preheat the oven to 350ºF. Mix together the bread crumbs, currants, pine nuts, capers, olives, parsley and mint, olive oil, and salt and pepper. Taste; even though the stuffing is still raw, you've got to get an idea of how much salt is needed.

2 Put the pepper halves into an ovenproof dish and spoon the stuffing into them. Drizzle olive oil over the top and bake for 1 hour. Serve hot or leave to cool to room temperature.

and also...

roasted peppers with tomatoes, mozzarella, and basil

Preheat the oven to 350ºF. Halve and seed 6 red bell peppers, then put ½ garlic clove, thinly sliced, and 2 to 3 cherry tomatoes in each half. Drizzle with olive oil, season with salt and pepper, and roast for 40 minutes. Put a thick slice of mozzarella on top of each pepper half, drizzle with more oil, and roast for 10 minutes, until the mozzarella has melted. Serve each pepper half topped with a slug of extra virgin olive oil, a sprinkle of freshly ground black pepper, and a sprinkle of torn basil leaves.

You can make this with broccoli rabe or ordinary broccoli, because the season for purple-sprouting is, sadly, so short. With its little leaves and mauve heads, purple-sprouting broccoli is enjoyed as much as asparagus, and you can treat it in similar ways. Eat it with melted butter or dip it into a soft-boiled egg.

A salad of warm purple-sprouting broccoli drizzled with a little balsamic vinegar and extra virgin olive oil and topped with shavings of Parmesan and a poached egg is also delicious. Broccoli stands up well to strong flavors, such as anchovy.

If you don't want to cook it with anchovies, as in the second recipe, steam and then toss with vinaigrette into which you have snipped some cured anchovies.

· · · · · ·

purple-sprouting broccoli with red pepper and garlic

serves 4 as a side dish

12 oz purple-sprouting broccoli

5 tbsp olive oil

4 cloves garlic, thinly sliced

¾ tsp dried red pepper flakes

salt and pepper

5 tbsp dry vermouth or dry white wine

extra virgin olive oil, to drizzle (optional)

1 Snip the rough ends off the broccoli and cut the larger pieces in half lengthwise. Remove any little leaves that don't look fresh.

2 Heat the olive oil in a frying pan or sauté pan and add the broccoli. Stir-fry for about 3 minutes, over high heat first of all, and then turn down to medium; it's just nice to get a little searing on the broccoli. Add the garlic and red pepper flakes and cook until the garlic is pale gold. Season with salt and pepper and add the vermouth. Let the vermouth bubble a little, then cover with a lid, and let the broccoli finish cooking in the steam created by the vermouth. Cook until just tender — about 4 minutes, but it does depend on the thickness of your broccoli, so check by piercing a stem with a sharp knife. Serve drizzled with a little extra virgin olive oil.

and also...

purple-sprouting broccoli with anchovy cream
Cook the broccoli as above, but just before you add the vermouth, push the broccoli to one side of the pan and add 8 anchovy fillets. Cook the anchovies, mashing them with your spoon, until they've started to disintegrate. Pour on some dry white wine instead of vermouth — about ⅓ cup — and finish as above.

autumn and
winter veggies

. . . . . .

Most recipes for roasted parsnips call for them to be parboiled before being roasted. I can rarely be bothered so I roast them raw, but it does mean that you need to use parsnips that aren't too old and woody.

. . . . . .

ginger, orange, and honey roasted parsnips

serves 4 as a side dish

1 lb parsnips

1 large onion

2 tbsp unsalted butter

juice of ½ orange

½ cup honey

2 tsp ground ginger

leaves from 4 sprigs thyme

salt and pepper

I Preheat the oven to 350°F. Trim the parsnips. Halve them and quarter the larger ones. Halve the onion and cut each piece into half-moon-shaped slices, about ½ inch thick at the thickest part.

2 Put the parsnips and onion in an ovenproof dish or roasting pan, and dot with little chunks of butter. Mix the orange juice with the honey and ginger. Pour two-thirds of this over the vegetables, add the thyme, and season well with salt and pepper.

3 Roast for 30 minutes, then pour over the rest of the orange juice mix, and put back in the oven. Roast for another 20 to 30 minutes. The parsnips should be soft, with caramelized tips, and the juice should have been absorbed. Serve immediately.

The Scandinavians pair the warm sweetness of beets with the saltiness of smoked fish. This dish is lovely with boiled little waxy potatoes and fillets of hot-smoked trout or salmon, or with baked fresh salmon.

· · · · · ·

swedish baked beets with onions, sour cream, and dill

serves 4 to 6 as a side dish

1½ lbs beets (try to get small ones)

¼ cup olive oil

salt and pepper

2 red onions, cut into half-moon-shaped wedges

⅔ cup sour cream

1 tbsp coarsely chopped fresh dill

I Preheat the oven to 350°F. Wrap the unpeeled beets in an aluminum foil packet, leaving an opening. Drizzle with half the olive oil, season with salt and pepper, close the packet, and put in a roasting pan. Roast until tender. How long this takes depends on the size of your beets — it could take as long as 1½ hours. Put the onion wedges in a small roasting pan, drizzle with the rest of the olive oil, season with salt and pepper, and roast in the same oven for 20 to 30 minutes. The onions should be tender and slightly singed at the tips.

2 When the beets are tender, peel each one (or leave the skin on if you prefer) and quarter or halve, depending on their size. Season the beets and put on a serving dish with the onions. Daub the sour cream over the vegetables and sprinkle with the dill. Serve hot or at room temperature.

potatoes without end...

If you're tired or short of time, tossing a green salad is the minimum amount of effort you need to make to ensure you get your veggie fix. But I love carbs, and they always take a bit more time. I roast potatoes drizzled with olive oil, or bake them in a whole host of ways. Potatoes are brilliant at absorbing different flavors, and I never stop feeling delighted that you put something as basic as spuds in the oven and, 30 minutes later, take out a lovely, golden dish of food. You have to use a roasting pan or ovenproof dish in which your potatoes can lie in a single layer. I use a metal roasting pan or a cast-iron Le Creuset gratin dish because they both conduct heat well.

rosemary, garlic, and olive oil roasted potatoes

serves 4

1½ lbs small new potatoes, cut into chunks about the size of a walnut

¼ cup olive oil

1 tbsp balsamic vinegar

2 garlic bulbs, cloves separated, unpeeled

6 branches fresh rosemary, leaves of half removed from the stems

salt and pepper

You can use small new potatoes, waxy varieties, or baking potatoes; they'll give you different but equally good results. Adapt the recipe by adding different spices — smoked paprika, dried red pepper flakes, or ground cumin and coriander — and omitting the rosemary. Add softer vegetables — chunks of eggplant, zucchini, or halved tomatoes — after the first 10 minutes of roasting time and toss them around in the oil too.

● Preheat the oven to 400°F. Mix all the ingredients together in a shallow ovenproof dish or roasting pan. The potatoes need to lie in a single layer. Roast for 35 minutes, or until the potatoes are tender. Give the dish a good shake from time to time to make sure all the sides get a bit of browning.

balsamic roasted potatoes and mushrooms

This is particularly good with grilled duck or steak.

● Preheat the oven to 400°F. Put the potatoes into a shallow ovenproof dish, leaving enough room for the mushrooms later. Pour over half the oil and half the vinegar, season with salt and pepper, and mix with your hands. Add the thyme and roast for 15 minutes. Add the mushrooms and the rest of the oil and vinegar, season again, and stir everything around. It looks as if there are too many mushrooms, but they will shrink. Roast for another 15 minutes or so, stirring twice more, until the potatoes are tender and dark.

serves 6

1½ lbs small waxy potatoes, halved

7 tbsp olive oil

3 tbsp balsamic vinegar

salt and pepper

about 6 branches thyme

8 large flat field or button mushrooms, cleaned and cut into thick slices

drunken potatoes

serves 6

2 lbs small waxy potatoes

½ cup chicken stock

½ cup white wine

1 tbsp salted butter

freshly ground
black pepper

a small handful of
finely chopped fresh
flat-leaf parsley

Another blueprint recipe, this one for baking potatoes in stock. Adapt it by using red wine and a couple of tbsp of olive oil instead of butter, and adding a few tsp of crushed coriander seeds and a bay leaf, and you have drunken potatoes, Greek style. I don't add salt to these because the reduced chicken stock provides enough.

• Preheat the oven to 400°F. Halve the potatoes and put them in a roasting pan or ovenproof dish. Heat the stock and wine together with the butter until boiling and pour over the potatoes. Season with pepper. Bake for 45 minutes. You'll need to turn the potatoes over halfway through the baking time. The liquid should have been completely absorbed by the end; cook for a little longer if it isn't. Sprinkle with the parsley and serve.

baked potatoes with chorizo

serves 6

2 lbs small waxy potatoes

3 onions

1 cup chicken stock

a good pinch of saffron strands

freshly ground black pepper

8 oz chorizo, skin removed, cut into slices about ⅛ inch thick

a small handful of finely chopped fresh parsley or cilantro

This is very good with meaty fish such as monkfish. The Spanish love chorizo and other pork products with fish. The combination works well.

• Preheat the oven to 400°F. Halve the potatoes and put them in a shallow ovenproof dish or roasting pan. Halve the onions, cut each half into four wedges, and add them too. Heat the chicken stock with the saffron and, once it's boiling, pour it over the vegetables. Season with pepper. Bake for 45 minutes, stirring the vegetables around, and adding the chorizo halfway through the baking time. The vegetables should be tender and the stock should have been absorbed by the end of the baking time. If there is still liquid left, then bake a little longer. Sprinkle with the parsley and serve.

baked potatoes with orange

serves 6

2 lbs small waxy potatoes

4 onions

½ cup chicken stock

⅓ cup orange juice

1 tbsp salted butter

2 tbsp marmalade

10 juniper seeds, crushed

freshly ground black pepper

Great with roast lamb or duck, or grilled duck breast.

• Preheat the oven to 400°F. Halve the potatoes and put them in a roasting pan or ovenproof dish. Halve the onions, cut each half into four wedges, and add them too. Heat the stock, orange juice, butter, and marmalade together, helping the marmalade melt by pressing it with the back of a spoon. Bring to a boil and pour over the potatoes. Sprinkle the juniper seeds over the top and season with pepper. Bake for 50 to 60 minutes, stirring the potatoes around halfway through the baking time. When done, the potatoes should be tender and golden and the liquid absorbed.

Excellent with smoked sausages in the winter, especially if you stir in some caraway seeds (fried in a little butter first) instead of the dill. This is also good with warm or cold poached salmon in the spring and summer.

. . . . . .

scandinavian potatoes in sour cream

serves 4 to 6

2¼ lbs small, waxy potatoes

6 tbsp hot chicken stock

6 tbsp sour cream

a couple of fronds of dill, chopped

a good squeeze of lemon

salt and pepper

I Cook the potatoes in boiling salted water until just tender. There's no need to peel them unless you really want to.

2 Drain the potatoes and add the stock, sour cream, dill, lemon juice, and salt and pepper. Mix gently, making sure that all the potatoes are nicely coated. Put into a warmed bowl and serve.

I wanted an easy accompaniment for Indian meat dishes. This seemed like the most hassle-free option. It's so good that I now serve the vegetables as a meal in their own right, with rice, chutneys, and plain yogurt.

. . . . . .

roasted vegetables with indian spices

serves 6

2 sweet potatoes, peeled and cut into large chunks

12 oz carrots, trimmed and halved lengthwise

1 butternut squash, peeled, seeded, and cut into long wedges

2 large onions, each one cut into 6 wedges

1 tbsp ground cumin

1½ tsp ground coriander

1 tbsp ground chile powder

1 tsp ground ginger

salt and pepper

6 tbsp sunflower oil

1 bunch cilantro, leaves coarsely chopped

I Preheat the oven to 375°F. Put everything except the cilantro in a single layer in a large roasting pan and mix together with your hands. Roast for 45 minutes, or until tender, turning the vegetables every so often. Sprinkle on the cilantro leaves before serving.

This is the kind of dish I usually hate. It mixes elements from completely different cuisines — a Thai-inspired dressing with Greek-style yogurt — but it works. It's such a satisfying mixture of hot, sour, salty, and sweet, and a contrast of temperatures too. Once you've eaten it, you'll crave it. The potatoes are good on their own with just a green salad, or as an accompaniment to roasted or grilled chicken.

• • • • • •

baked sweet potato with cilantro and chile relish

serves 4

4 sweet potatoes

¾ cup plain Greek-style yogurt

relish

3 tbsp fresh cilantro leaves

3 cloves garlic

juice of 1 lime

1 tsp superfine sugar

2 tbsp olive oil

½-inch square piece fresh ginger, peeled and grated

¾ tsp Asian fish sauce

1 medium fresh red chile, halved, seeded, and finely chopped

I Preheat the oven to 375°F. You don't need to prepare the sweet potatoes in any way. Bake them for about 45 minutes, depending on size, until tender when pierced with a skewer.

2 While the potatoes are cooking, put all the ingredients for the relish (except the chile) in a blender and puree.

3 Split the potatoes down the middle lengthwise, as you would a regular baked potato, and spoon some yogurt inside. Add the chile to the relish, then spoon some of this on top of the yogurt and serve.

and also...

baked sweet potato with goat cheese and olive and walnut relish

Bake the sweet potatoes as above and, while they're baking, put ½ cup walnut pieces, a garlic clove, and a small handful of chopped fresh flat-leaf parsley into a mortar. Pound with a pestle, gradually adding 2 tbsp extra virgin olive oil, until you have a coarse, thick paste. Add the chopped flesh of 1¼ cups black olives and pound again, but don't beat the olives into a paste — they should still have some texture. Stir in a good squeeze of lemon juice and season. Split the sweet potatoes down the middle and divide 6 oz crumbled goat cheese among them. Spoon some of the walnut and olive relish on top.

This always looks so good — a big dish of golden and tawny vegetables with singed tips — and requires no care whatsoever. You can add chunks of sweet potato, slices of squash, and halved small beets to the mixture, and flavor with rosemary or sage instead of thyme.

. . . . . .

roasted autumn vegetables

serves 6

1½ lbs small waxy potatoes or larger baking potatoes

1 lb carrots, trimmed and halved lengthwise if large

1 lb parsnips, trimmed and halved lengthwise

3 red onions, each cut into 6 wedges

¼ cup olive oil

1 tbsp balsamic vinegar

leaves from a couple of sprigs of thyme, plus 5 whole sprigs

salt and pepper

I Preheat the oven to 375°F. Cut the potatoes into chunks about the size of a walnut, though some waxy varieties are very small and may not need to be cut. Put all the vegetables into a large roasting pan — they should be able to lie in a single layer — and add the olive oil, vinegar, thyme leaves, and salt and pepper. Toss everything together with your hands.

2 Roast for 45 to 60 minutes, until the vegetables are tender. Give them a shake every so often, and add the whole thyme sprigs halfway through the cooking time. Cover the dish with aluminum foil if some of the vegetables are getting too dark, though it's good if some of them end up slightly charred at the tips.

and also...

maple and mustard roasted vegetables
Make as above and spoon ¼ cup dark maple syrup mixed with ¼ cup coarse-grain mustard evenly over the vegetables 10 minutes before the end of roasting time.

roasted jerusalem artichokes with onions, lemon, and thyme
Take 1 lb Jerusalem artichokes — cut off the more knobbly bits and wash well, but don't peel them — and halve the larger ones lengthwise. Put into a roasting pan with 2 onions, cut into wedges. Throw in 6 sprigs of thyme, the juice of 1 lemon, and 5 tbsp olive oil. Season with salt and pepper and toss around with your hands. Roast as above.

This is adapted from a recipe in Claudia Roden's fabulous *A Book of Middle Eastern Food*. I usually eat it with plain rice or couscous and yogurt as an easy midweek supper.

. . . . . .

middle eastern lentils and peppers

serves 4 as a main course

¼ cup olive oil

1 large leek, washed and cut into rounds

1 red bell pepper, halved, seeded, and sliced

1½ tsp ground cumin

2 tsp ground coriander

1 fresh red chile, seeded and chopped (or hot pepper sauce)

1 cup red lentils

1¼ cups water or stock (a bouillon cube is fine)

1 (14-oz) can tomatoes in puree

1 tsp sugar

1 tbsp tomato paste

salt and pepper

a large handful of cilantro leaves, coarsely chopped

I Heat the olive oil in a heavy-bottomed saucepan and add the leek and bell pepper. Cook for about 10 minutes, until soft. Stir in the spices and cook for 2 minutes, then add all the other ingredients except the cilantro and simmer over a gentle heat for about 25 minutes, until the lentils have collapsed. Taste for seasoning and stir in the cilantro. Serve with plain yogurt or tzatziki (see page 49).

Poor onions: always in the chorus line, never the star. Well, not here. A dish for all those who fight over the one onion that roasts inside the chicken. (Isn't that everyone?)

. . . . . .

melting roast onions

serves 6 as a side dish

6 (5-oz) onions, skins on

¼ cup olive oil

salt and pepper

¼ cup salted butter

I Preheat the oven to 375°F. Trim the bottom of the onions without removing the root. Cut a deep cross from the top to three-quarters of the way down each and rub them all over with olive oil, then season with salt and pepper. Sit them snugly in a small ovenproof dish. Cover with aluminum foil.

2 Roast for 70 minutes. Remove the foil, divide the butter among the onions, and roast for 25 minutes, basting with the melted butter a few times. Serve at once.

and also...

melting roast onions with cheese
Roast the onions as above, then grate or slice 6 oz cheese and stuff it into the center of the onions. Roast until the cheese melts for a great supper dish.

Tarka dhal shouldn't be too heavily flavored; it is a mild background against which to highlight more strongly spiced food, and here the onions provide that. There's enough to serve two as a main course with chutneys, rice, and plain yogurt, or serve as a side dish with an Indian spiced meat or chicken dish.

· · · · · ·

tarka dhal with crisp onions

serves 4 as a side dish

1¼ cups red lentils

½ tsp ground turmeric

1¾-inch square piece fresh ginger, peeled and finely chopped

salt and pepper

¼ cup sunflower oil

1 large onion, very thinly sliced

2 cloves garlic, finely chopped

1½ tsp ground coriander

1 tbsp ground cumin

½ tsp cayenne pepper

juice of ½ small lemon

a fistful of cilantro leaves, coarsely chopped

I Put the lentils into a pan with the turmeric, ginger, and salt and pepper; cover with water (about 2¼ cups). Bring to a boil and partly cover with a lid. Turn the heat down and simmer the lentils for about 30 minutes. They should melt into a puree (you don't want the lentils to be too thick, so do add more water if you need to).

2 In the meantime, heat 3 tbsp of the sunflower oil and fry the onion over medium-high heat for about 10 minutes; the edges should brown nicely. Add the rest of the oil and throw in the garlic, coriander, cumin, and cayenne. Toss the onion around with the flavorings for a couple of minutes.

3 Season the lentils with salt, pepper, and lemon juice. Pour into a warm serving dish and sprinkle the onion and the cilantro on top.

Roasted, the tips of carrots, parsnips, and onions caramelize, and the flavor of beets intensifies. And just look at those colors!

serves 4 as a side dish

2 lbs winter squash or pumpkin

¼ cup olive oil

2 tbsp salted butter

4 sprigs thyme

salt and pepper

6 cloves garlic, thinly sliced

Use the sweeter varieties of squash or pumpkin for this. The pale-green-skinned Kabucha has a great flavor, and butternut squash is also very dependable.

· · · · · ·

roasted squash with garlic and thyme

I Preheat the oven to 375ºF. Halve the squash and scoop out and discard the seeds and fibers. Cut into slices about ¾ inch thick at the thickest part. Put the olive oil and butter in a shallow roasting pan and heat gently. Add the wedges of squash. Pull the leaves off the thyme and sprinkle those on, seasoning with salt and pepper. Turn the wedges over, making sure you get herbs, fat, and seasoning all over them. Roast for 30 to 35 minutes, or until tender and slightly caramelized. Baste the squash pieces every so often while they're cooking and sprinkle the garlic over 15 minutes before the end of cooking time.

and also...

roasted squash with chile and ginger
Make as above, but sprinkle the squash slices with 2 fresh shredded red chiles (halved and seeded first) and finely chopped ginger (peel and chop a 2-inch square of fresh ginger) 15 minutes before the end of cooking time.

Mmmm . . . fennel! This is a really fragrant treat but it is fairly rich so I always like to serve it with something quite plain, such as roast or grilled chicken or lamb.

· · · · · ·

fennel and gruyère gratin

serves 4 as a side dish, 2 as a main course

4 fennel bulbs, trimmed of discolored outer leaves

salt and pepper

1 cup heavy cream

¼ cup grated Gruyère cheese

¼ cup grated Parmesan cheese

I Preheat the oven to 400°F. Trim the fennel tops and save any feathery fronds for later. Quarter each bulb lengthwise and cook the pieces in lightly salted boiling water for 4 to 5 minutes, until nearly tender when pierced with the tip of a sharp knife. Drain well and lay the fennel in a buttered gratin dish, then sprinkle any reserved fronds on top. Season with salt and pepper, pour on the cream, and sprinkle with the cheeses. Bake for 20 minutes.

Not all autumn and winter vegetable dishes need to be cooked to softness and sweetness. Salads are also good, as long as they are not too delicate. This one is great for serving with fish or lamb.

· · · · · ·

warm potato, fennel, and olive salad

serves 6

2 lbs small waxy potatoes

2 fennel bulbs

24 good-quality black olives

5 tbsp extra virgin olive oil

juice of ½ lemon

salt and pepper

I Cook the potatoes in boiling salted water until tender. While they're cooking, remove any tough outer leaves from the fennel and trim the tops, retaining any feathery fronds. Halve the fennel lengthwise and remove the little hard core from each piece and discard. Cut the fennel into very thin slices. Chop the reserved fronds.

2 When the potatoes are tender, drain well, and toss while still warm with the fennel, chopped fronds, olives, oil, and lemon juice. Season with salt and pepper. Serve warm or at room temperature.

Spanish cuisine boasts lots of bean dishes, slow-cooked with smoky chorizo, but they take ages. This one is good when you crave those textures and flavors without the wait.

· · · · · ·

white beans and cabbage with chorizo

serves 4

8 oz Savoy cabbage, about ½ medium-sized head

¼ cup olive oil

2 cloves garlic, sliced

1 fresh red chile, halved, seeded, and thinly sliced

6 oz chorizo, skin removed and cut into slices

1 (14-oz) can cannellini beans, drained and rinsed

salt and pepper

I Cut the cabbage in half. Remove the tough central white core from each piece and cut the leaves into slices about the thickness of your thumb.

2 Put half the olive oil into a frying pan with a lid. Add the garlic, chile, and chorizo and sauté until the garlic is pale gold and the chorizo colored evenly. Toss in the cabbage and beans with the rest of the oil and season with salt and pepper. Stir the vegetables, then add a good splash of water. Turn down the heat, cover the pan, and leave for 3 minutes, then give it all a stir and check that the beans are hot. Serve at once.

These smart beans are the perfect accompaniment for roast lamb or lamb chops. They're lovely with a couple of tablespoons of heavy cream stirred in and warmed through as well.

· · · · · ·

flageolet beans with garlic and parsley

serves 6 as a side dish

1½ tbsp salted butter

2 cloves garlic, finely chopped

2 (14-oz) cans flageolet or cannellini beans, drained and rinsed

2 tbsp finely chopped fresh flat-leaf parsley

salt and pepper

I Melt the butter in a large saucepan and gently sauté the garlic until soft (just a couple of minutes). Add the beans, parsley, and plenty of salt and pepper. Stir everything together until heated through.

spring and
summer fruit
• • • • • • •

Any red berries are good, particularly raspberries and loganberries. Currants and even blueberries work well too.

• • • • • •

summer berry brûlée

serves 6

1½ lbs mixed raspberries and red and black currants

½ cup superfine sugar

1¼ cups heavy cream

1¼ cups Greek-style yogurt

¾ cup granulated sugar

I Put the fruit into a gratin dish (one that can take the heat of a broiler) and sprinkle half the superfine sugar all over it. Whip the cream and blend it with the yogurt and the rest of the superfine sugar. Spread the cream over the fruit. Cover with plastic wrap and put in the refrigerator to chill well (the cream mixture firms up, which is really important).

2 Dust the granulated sugar evenly over the top of the cream and turn your broiler to its highest setting. Broil the dish so that the sugar on top caramelizes — you may have to move it around a bit because most broilers tend to be hotter in some patches and colder in others. Try to get it as evenly caramelized as possible. Remove from the broiler and let it come to room temperature. The sugar will set to a delicious crisp, sugary sheet — shiny and smooth enough to skate on — that contrasts brilliantly with the fruit.

Sometimes you want a dessert just
because of the idea of it.
This is one of them: golden eggy bread,
tart raspberries, rich cream. . . .
Irresistible. If you can't get your hands
on brioche — the sweet French
bread — any good white bread will do
as long as it has a soft crust.

· · · · · ·

pain perdu with crème fraîche and raspberries

serves 4

⅔ cup heavy cream

2 large eggs, plus 1 large egg yolk

2 tbsp sugar

8 medium slices brioche

¼ cup unsalted butter

confectioners' sugar, for dusting

8 oz raspberries

crème fraîche, to serve

I Whisk the cream, eggs, and sugar together. Either leave the brioche slices whole or cut them in half (a stack of four halves can look very good). Dunk the first two slices of brioche in the egg mix and leave for 5 minutes.

2 Melt a pat of the butter in a frying pan and cook the brioche slices, a couple at a time, adding more butter as you need to, until golden on each side. You need to dunk the next slices of brioche in the egg mixture as you go along. Put each slice on a paper towel as it is cooked.

3 Serve two slices of brioche per person, sift confectioners' sugar over each serving, and add the raspberries and crème fraîche.

This is a very popular summer dessert in Sweden, where it's made with an almond paste called *mandelmass*. Marzipan works well instead, and you can use blueberries instead of raspberries.

· · · · · ·

swedish baked peaches and raspberries with almonds

serves 6

8 ripe peaches, halved and pitted

8 oz raspberries

⅓ cup booze (ideally amaretto, Marsala, peach schnapps, or even Cointreau)

juice of ½ small orange

2 tbsp granulated sugar

7 oz marzipan

1 tbsp flaked almonds

confectioners' sugar, to serve

crème fraîche or Greek-style yogurt, to serve

I Preheat the oven to 375°F. Cut each peach half into quarters and put them into a dish where they can be packed tightly together. Sprinkle the raspberries on top and pour on the alcohol and the orange juice. Sprinkle on half the granulated sugar. Pull the marzipan into little nuggets, then sprinkle those on top of the fruit, followed by the rest of the granulated sugar and the flaked almonds.

2 Bake for 30 to 35 minutes. The peaches should be tender and slightly caramelized in patches. Leave to cool and serve warm or at room temperature, dusted lightly with confectioners' sugar and accompanied by the crème fraîche.

You can use raspberries for this dish as well as strawberries. Basil's perfume goes well with them both.

· · · · · ·

strawberries and pineapple in basil syrup

serves 6

1 cup superfine sugar

2 strips lemon zest

3¼ cups water

4 large sprigs basil, torn, plus more sprigs to serve

1 ripe pineapple

1 lb strawberries

juice of ½ lemon

I Gently heat the sugar and lemon zest strips in the water, until the sugar has dissolved; boil for 15 minutes. Remove from the heat, add the basil, and let the syrup infuse and cool.

2 Remove the skin from the pineapple and cut the flesh into rounds. Divide each round into six little segments, removing the hard central core. Make sure that you remove any discolored bits and any little bits of skin. Hull the strawberries and halve or quarter the larger ones.

3 Put the fruit into a serving bowl. Add the lemon juice to the basil syrup, then strain the syrup over the fruit. Put a sprig of fresh basil on top and serve.

A play on Eton Mess, that very English confection of crushed meringue, strawberries, and cream.

· · · · · ·

strawberry and passion fruit mess

serves 6

1 lb strawberries

7 passion fruit

1¼ cups heavy cream

¾ cup Greek-style yogurt

juice of 1 lime

½ cup confectioners' sugar

4 oz meringue cookies

I Hull the strawberries and quarter or halve the largest ones. Halve the passion fruit and extract the flesh and seeds from all of them. Whip the cream, then add the yogurt, lime juice, and sugar. Stir the strawberries and the passion fruit flesh and seeds (keeping back the smallest strawberries and some passion fruit for decoration) into the cream.

2 Coarsely smash up the meringues and gently fold them into the cream. Pile into glasses and garnish each one with a small strawberry and a drizzle of passion fruit. Serve immediately.

serves 6

3¼ cups white wine

¾ cup sugar

2 strips lemon zest

juice of ½ lemon

6 peaches, white ones if you can get them

2 tsp rose water, or to taste

to serve

a small handful of pistachios, coarsely chopped

deep-red rose petals, shredded or torn

Peaches are beautiful with pistachios and roses, so this is a gorgeous-looking dish. If you have perfectly ripe peaches that aren't too big, they'll look good left whole, but halve and pit them if you prefer — it does make the cooking time quicker.

• • • • • •

peaches in rose syrup

I Put the wine, sugar, and lemon zest and juice into a saucepan big enough to hold the peaches as well. Bring gently to a boil, stirring from time to time to help the sugar dissolve.

2 Leave the peaches whole and add them to the wine mixture. Poach gently, turning them over every so often, until they are just tender. The length of time this takes depends on how ripe the peaches are. Remove the peaches and boil the poaching liquid until it is reduced and slightly syrupy. Leave to cool — the liquid will thicken more as it cools — then add the rose water.

3 Carefully remove the skins from the peaches (they should just slip off) and halve them. Pour the syrup over the cooked peaches and chill. Throw some chopped pistachios and shredded rose petals over the top and serve.

and also...

peaches in white wine and basil

Make as above, but add a small bunch of basil leaves to the poaching liquid, then remove them once the syrup has cooled, and use fresh leaves for serving. The basil flavor works well with red as well as white wine.

Offer me baked apricots or half a dozen fancy pastries, and I will choose the former every time. Apricots can be rather mealy and lacking in flavor, but the wine, vanilla, sugar, and heat somehow seem to reach into them and bring out their wonderful tart "honeyedness."
Use good-quality vanilla extract, if you don't have a pod. It won't look as pretty, but it will still taste good.

• • • • • •

vanilla-baked apricots

serves 4

16 apricots, halved and pitted

1⅛ cups white wine

1 vanilla pod, or 2 tsp pure vanilla extract

½ cup sugar

whipped cream, crème fraîche, or sweetened Greek-style yogurt, to serve

Italian cookies, to serve

I Preheat the oven to 350°F. Lay the apricots, skin-side up, in overlapping circles or rows in an ovenproof dish. Pour on the wine.

2 Split the vanilla pod and scrape out the seeds. Tuck the pod under the fruit and add the seeds to the white wine, agitating the dish to distribute them. Sprinkle with the sugar.

3 Bake for 20 to 25 minutes, or until the apricots are tender and the sugar is very slightly caramelized. Allow to cool, then chill.

4 Serve with whipped cream and little Italian cookies (amaretti or biscotti).

and also...

cardamom-baked apricots
Make as above, but add the seeds from 6 cardamom pods to the wine and omit the vanilla. This is delicious served with plain Greek-style yogurt drizzled with a little honey and sprinkled with pistachios.

lavender-baked apricots
Add 3 sprigs of fresh lavender to the wine and use fresh sprigs for serving. You can also replace some of the sugar with lavender honey.

apricots in marsala
Replace the white wine with dry Marsala.

You can add blackberries or black currants to the cooked fruit before serving. I like this best served with a big bowl of sweetened mascarpone cheese mixed with Greek-style yogurt.

• • • • • • •

cassis-baked fruit

serves 6

2 peaches or nectarines

4 plums

8 apricots

2 small apples

¾ cup red wine

¾ cup crème de cassis (black currant liqueur)

4½ tbsp sugar

1 Preheat the oven to 325ºF. Halve all the stone fruits. Cut the peaches into eighths and the plums into quarters. Core the apples and cut each half into six segments; I don't bother to peel them because I like the texture of the skin in the finished dish. Put the fruit into a shallow ovenproof dish and add the wine, liqueur, and sugar.

2 Bake for 50 minutes, stirring a couple of times if you get the chance.

When I was a teenager, one of my mother's most elegant friends produced, for dessert, a bowl of ripe peaches, a pitcher of cream, and a silver sugar shaker. We watched as she carefully peeled her peach, sliced it, drizzled it with cream, dusted it with sugar, and ate. It seemed like the perfect way to end a meal. With good food, it is sometimes best to do very little.

You can spend all summer never cooking a dessert at all, just serving fresh fruit. But as the months progress, fruit becomes abundant enough to take a less puristic approach. Keep it simple, though. Poached or baked fruit with subtle flavorings, such as flower waters or herbs, make the best eating.

Don't use rock-hard apricots here; you can bake hard apricots to softness but broiling them won't work. Keep the apricots in a bowl until they're tender. You can use blueberries if you can't find blackberries.

. . . . . .

broiled apricots with blackberries and mascarpone

serves 4

12 ripe apricots, halved and pitted

6 tbsp superfine sugar

⅔ cup mascarpone cheese

½ cup blackberries

I Preheat the broiler. Put the apricot halves, skin-side down, in a dish that can take the heat of a broiler (such as a Le Creuset gratin dish). Sprinkle on a third of the sugar. Spoon the mascarpone into the hollows of the apricots and sprinkle the berries on and around the apricots. Sprinkle on another third of the sugar and put the dish under a very hot broiler. Broil for 3 minutes. Sprinkle on the rest of the sugar and broil for another 3 minutes. The top should be glazed and bubbling. Serve immediately.

Gooseberries and elderflowers were
made for each other, so here is
the taste of heaven in a good
old-fashioned crumble.

. . . . . .

gooseberry and almond crumble with elderflower cream

serves 8

2 lbs gooseberries, topped and tailed

⅔ cup superfine sugar

1 cup all-purpose flour

1⅛ cups ground almonds

¾ cup salted butter, chopped

⅓ cup flaked almonds

elderflower cream (see opposite page), to serve

1 Preheat the oven to 350°F. Put the gooseberries in an ovenproof serving bowl, and stir in 3 tbsp of the superfine sugar. Add ¼ cup water.

2 To make the crumble, mix the flour, the rest of the sugar, and the ground almonds together. Rub in the butter until the mixture turns crumbly. Put the crumble on top of the gooseberries, sprinkle the flaked almonds over the top, and bake for about 40 minutes. The top of the crumble should be golden. Leave to cool.

3 Serve with elderflower cream.

and also...

raspberry, apple, and almond crumble
Make as above, with 4 tart apples (peel and core them) and 1 lb raspberries. Also good with elderflower cream, though you could try adding a little framboise — raspberry liqueur — to the cream instead of elderflower cordial.

Delicious with clouds of meringue or good-quality shortbread. You can also make an orange or lemon cream by mixing the yogurt and cream with store-bought orange or lemon curd.

· · · · · ·

poached rhubarb with elderflower cream

serves 4 to 6

2 lbs rhubarb

1¼ cups water

¾ cup sugar

a good squeeze of lemon juice

elderflower cream

1 cup Greek-style yogurt

½ cup heavy cream

¾ cup confectioners' sugar

a good squeeze of lemon juice

about 3 tbsp elderflower cordial (available online), or to taste

I Trim the rhubarb and cut it into 2½-inch lengths. Mix the water, sugar, and lemon juice and heat, stirring from time to time, until the sugar has dissolved. Add the rhubarb to the sugar syrup and poach gently until just soft (the rhubarb must not collapse). Remove the rhubarb carefully with a slotted spoon and boil the poaching liquid to reduce it. The liquid should be slightly syrupy. Leave to cool and then add to the rhubarb. It's lovely chilled, so put it in the refrigerator.

2 To make the elderflower cream, beat the yogurt and heavy cream together until blended. Add the confectioners' sugar, lemon juice, and elderflower cordial and mix well. (The cream will thicken when you add the lemon juice, but you will balance this out when you add the cordial. You should end up with a mixture that is firm but not stiff.) Cover and keep in the refrigerator until needed.

3 Serve the rhubarb in broad, shallow bowls, such as soup plates, with a good dollop of the cream.

A very grown-up dessert.

. . . . . .

raspberry and beaujolais granita

serves 8

1¼ lbs raspberries
¾ cup superfine sugar
¾ cup Beaujolais

I Toss the raspberries in a bowl with ¼ cup of the sugar. Leave for an hour. Heat the rest of the sugar in a saucepan with 10 tbsp of the wine, stirring to help the sugar dissolve. Boil for 2 minutes, then leave to cool.

2 Puree the berries in a food processor. Push the puree through a sieve. Mix with the cooled syrup and the remaining wine. Chill. Freeze in a broad, shallow container. After 1½ hours, fork the bit that has frozen around the edge of the dish into the rest of the liquid. Fork about three more times (every 1½ to 2 hours) during the freezing, which will take about 8 hours total. You want to break up the ice to make little shard-like crystals, not break them down as you would for a sorbet. If you make the granita the day before, put it in the refrigerator to defrost for about 20 minutes, then fork it again before serving.

and also...

gin and tonic granita
Gently heat 1¼ cups water and 1½ cups superfine sugar as above. Cool. Mix with the juice of 2 limes, the grated zest of 1 lime, 1⅔ cups tonic water, and ½ cup gin. Continue as above.

peach and prosecco granita
Make a sugar syrup as above, using 1¼ cups water and ¾ cup superfine sugar. Cool. Puree the flesh of 4 ripe peaches. Sieve and mix with the syrup, the juice of 1½ lemons, and 1⅔ cups Prosecco. Continue as above. This is delicious with crème de pêche (French peach liqueur) poured over each serving.

The best meals end with elegance and simplicity. These make perfect finales when you're short of time.

· · · · · ·

no-cook desserts

peaches with gorgonzola and mascarpone

This looks stunning and is a gorgeous combination of flavors. You need perfectly ripe, flavorful peaches (white-fleshed ones, if you can get them, are the most beautiful and scented). Leave some whole, halve or slice others, and serve them on a platter with a wedge of Gorgonzola cheese, a bowl of mascarpone cheese, and a generous chunk of honey on the comb.

peaches in moscato

A chic but lazy Italian dessert. Give every diner a glass of chilled Moscato (an Italian dessert wine, or French Muscat de Beaumes-de-Venise if you prefer) and a perfectly ripe peach. Let them peel their own peaches and cut them into slices, dropping each slice into the glass. Eat.

prosecco with sorbet and summer berries

Fill champagne glasses with chilled Prosecco (not too much because it will froth once you add the sorbet). Drop a few red berries into the glasses and carefully top each one with a scoop of sorbet — mango or berry are good. Very glamorous.

figs and raspberries with mascarpone

Sounds plain, but the beauty of fresh figs makes this luxurious. Serve the figs whole on a large plate with the berries surrounding them and a big bowl of mascarpone cheese drizzled with good honey.

labneh with honey, pistachios, and berries

Labneh is drained yogurt. For a sweet version you just mix plain Greek-style yogurt with some confectioners' sugar and put it in a muslin- or cheesecloth-lined sieve set over a bowl to drain overnight. Carefully remove the cloth and serve whole on a platter, or sliced into smaller wedges on individual plates. Drizzle with honey. Sprinkle with chopped pistachios and put red berries or slices of ripe peach, nectarine, or mango alongside.

strawberries in beaujolais

Hull and wash strawberries and halve the larger ones. Put into a broad, shallow bowl and pour on enough Beaujolais to soak without covering. Sprinkle with superfine sugar, gently stir, and leave to macerate for 30 minutes before serving. You can use Valpolicella or a mixture of orange juice and Cointreau instead.

cherries on ice

There's nothing to this but it really sings of summer. Just wash the cherries — leaving the stems on — and pile them into a bowl half-filled with ice cubes.

boozy raisins

Put good raisins — such as muscat or Chilean flame — into a big mason jar, leaving room for the fruit to expand as it plumps up. Pour over enough booze (it should be something sweet, such as Madeira or Marsala) to cover the fruit completely, put the lid on, and leave to plump up over a few days. Top up with more wine if the fruit starts to come up above the level of the liquid. Delicious with vanilla ice cream or big dollops of Greek-style yogurt or crème fraîche. Sprinkle each serving with toasted hazelnuts, pine nuts, or almonds.

apricots in sauternes

Another good standby to have stashed in the cupboard. Pour a bottle of Sauternes (or you can use Muscat de Beaumes-de-Venise, Moscato, or Moscatel) over 2 lbs dried apricots packed in a mason jar. Cover and leave for at least a couple of weeks before eating. Top up with more wine if the fruit starts to come up above the level of the liquid. Sprinkle with toasted flaked almonds or chopped pistachios before serving.

prunes in armagnac

Richer and more boozy than the apricots above, so serve in smaller portions. Put 2 lbs very good-quality prunes into a mason jar and cover with Armagnac or brandy. Cover and leave for at least a month before eating. You can do the same thing with dried figs. Both are great served alongside full-flavored cheeses.

chocolate-stuffed prunes

You can make these and stash them away, or prepare them very quickly. Get good-quality prunes. Make a slit in each one, remove the pit, and stuff with chunks of dark chocolate and half a shelled walnut or a blanched almond. Make them more complicated if you wish, adding chopped candied peel or nuggets of marzipan to the mixture. Leave the prunes as they are or dip them in melted dark chocolate and allow to set. Beautiful if you can be bothered to wrap each one in tissue paper (go for fuchsia or purple paper — gorgeous). Great with strong, dark espresso.

moroccan oranges with cinnamon

This only requires you to slice a few oranges but is a lovely, exotic, and scented end to a winter meal. Peel and slice the oranges according to the instructions on page 168. Lay the slices on a platter and pour any reserved juice over the top. Sprinkle with superfine sugar (but taste first to see whether the oranges need it or not) and a tbsp (or two — you

judge, but don't make it too perfumed) of orange-flower water. Sprinkle on a little ground cinnamon and chopped pistachios. Chill before serving.

figs with goat cheese

The soft, bloomy skin of figs goes very well with goat cheese. Make sure your figs are ripe and sweet and serve them whole, or cut them in quarters without cutting right through to the bottom so that they open out like flowers. Leave the goat cheese whole and serve on the same platter. Hazelnuts (shelled but not skinned) are lovely with this too, as is a good honey.

feta-stuffed dates

Good for finishing off a Middle Eastern or North African meal. Just pit fresh or dried dates and stuff a nugget of feta cheese inside each one. You can add some slivers of pistachio as well, if you want.

dark chocolate and sherry

You want really good-quality dark chocolate for this — something with more than 70 percent cocoa solids — and you should get a good brand such as Valrhona or Green and Black's. Be generous. Simple desserts need to be abundant or you just look like a cheapskate. Serve with glasses of Pedro Ximénez, a sweet dessert sherry that tastes gorgeously of burnt sugar and raisins.

affogato

A simple ice-cream sundae for grown-ups. Make really good strong coffee, preferably espresso. Put a scoop of very cold, good-quality vanilla ice cream into small bowls or coffee cups (it must be really cold). Pour a cupful of the hot coffee over the top of the ice cream and serve immediately. You can dress it up with a capful of liqueur, if you like (Galliano and amaretto are nice).

autumn and winter fruit

. . . . . .

One of the many apple desserts that are so popular in Scandinavia, this is from my Swedish friend, Johanna. It's not a tart, a crumble, or a crisp, but it is incredibly easy and delicious and about the quickest dessert you could make for weekend lunch.

· · · · · ·

johanna's swedish apple pie

serves 8

5 apples, peeled and cored

¾ cup sugar

1¾ cups all-purpose flour

¾ tsp baking powder

finely grated zest of 1 lemon

9 tbsp salted butter

½ cup flaked almonds

to finish

confectioners' sugar

I Preheat the oven to 400°F. Butter an ovenproof dish. Cut the apples into wedges and lay them in the dish. Mix the sugar, flour, baking powder, and lemon zest. Melt the butter and stir it into this, mixing well. Spread the mixture over the apples, and top with the almonds.

2 Bake for 30 minutes. Let cool slightly, then dust with confectioners' sugar, and serve.

Homely desserts — fat baked apples and juice-splattered crumbles — cheer everyone up. Why offer a store-bought cheesecake when a bowl of stewed apples and a pitcher of cream is so easy?

I generally find that baking apples are a bit large to serve as a dessert, but other apples are just the right size. You can fill them with honey, dried fruits, and nuts and pour fruit juice, hard cider, or sherry around them.

· · · · · ·

new england baked apples

serves 4

4 large apples

⅓ cup dried cranberries or raisins (or a mixture)

⅓ cup fresh cranberries

⅓ cup pecan pieces

½ cup maple syrup, plus extra for drizzling

⅔ cup hard cider or fruit juice

crème fraîche, to serve

I Preheat the oven to 350°F. Make a "lid" out of the top of each apple by cutting around the stem (make each one about 2 inches across). Set the lids aside and remove the core from the rest of the apple with a corer.

2 Mix together the dried and fresh cranberries, pecans, and maple syrup. Place the apples in an ovenproof dish and spoon the stuffing into them. Put the lids on and drizzle some maple syrup over each apple. Pour the cider into the dish around the apples. Bake for 30 to 40 minutes. The apples should be tender. Spoon the juice over the apples every so often while they are cooking. Serve warm, with crème fraîche.

and also...

marmalade-baked apples

Mix ¼ cup flaked almonds, ¼ cup golden or dark raisins, 3 tbsp marmalade, and 2 tbsp dark corn syrup and stir in the juice of ½ orange. Fill the apples as above, top with 1 tsp marmalade and 1 tbsp dark corn syrup. Pour the juice of 1½ oranges into the dish and bake as above.

swedish baked apples with tosca sauce

Preheat the oven to 400°F. Dot little pats of salted butter and sprinkle 2 tbsp sugar over 4 halved and cored apples and bake for 30 minutes. In a small saucepan, mix ¼ cup butter, ¼ cup sugar, 1 tbsp all-purpose flour, ⅔ cup flaked almonds, and ¼ cup heavy cream. Heat carefully, stirring until it thickens. Pour over the apples and bake for another 10 minutes, until they're tender and golden.

If you don't have stale cake on hand and can't find brioche, you can use any sweet bread or fruit loaf to make the crumbs for this.

. . . . . .

cranberry and apple brown betty

serves 6

1½ cups firmly packed light brown sugar

½ tsp ground apple pie spice and ½ tsp ground ginger

3 cups stale plain cake or brioche crumbs

8 tbsp salted butter, melted

1½ lbs apples, peeled, cored, and thinly sliced

10 oz fresh cranberries

4 oz dried cranberries

¼ cup orange juice

whipped cream or vanilla ice cream

I Preheat the oven to 350ºF. Mix the brown sugar and spices together. Put 3 tbsp into the crumbs and stir in the melted butter.

2 Toss the apples and cranberries with the rest of the sugar-and-spice mix. Butter a shallow pie dish and spread half the crumbs in the bottom. Pile the apples and cranberries on top and pour in the orange juice. Put the rest of the crumbs on top and bake, loosely covered with aluminum foil, for 20 minutes. Remove the foil and bake for another 20 minutes, until golden. Serve with whipped cream.

Fools can be rich so they're best made with tart fruit. You can use plums instead of apples, but taste carefully to adjust the amount of maple syrup.

. . . . . .

apple, maple, and ginger fool

serves 4

1¾ cups tart apples, peeled

2 tbsp water

2 tbsp light brown sugar

2 pieces preserved ginger in syrup, chopped, plus 1 tbsp ginger syrup from the jar

1¼ cups heavy cream

⅔ cup Greek-style yogurt

8 tbsp dark maple syrup, plus more for drizzling

I Cut the apples into chunks, discarding the cores, and put into a saucepan with the water and the brown sugar. Heat gently, then simmer until the apples are completely soft and mushy. Leave to cool.

2 Puree the apples with the ginger and ginger syrup. Whip the cream until it holds soft peaks. Carefully mix the apple puree, yogurt, custard, and maple syrup together and chill. Serve in a large bowl or in individual glasses, drizzled with maple syrup.

2 perfectly ripe, medium mangoes, peeled

6 passion fruit

juice of 4 limes and finely grated zest of 2 limes

superfine sugar

1¼ cups heavy cream

5 tbsp white rum

Thank goodness for tropical fruits: they're at their best during our winter months. Mangoes, which don't have much natural acidity, really sing out when teamed with the tartness of passion fruit or lime juice. You don't have to limit the combination to this dish, of course; mango and passion fruit are also great with cold rice pudding, or combined with segments of orange for a simple fruit compote to serve with whipped cream.

· · · · · ·

mangoes and passion fruit with rum and lime syllabub

I Cut off the "cheeks" of the mangoes by slicing through the flesh on either side of the central pit, so that you are left with two rounded fleshy sides and a pit, which still has quite a lot of fruit on it. Cut the cheeks into neat slices. Cut as much of the fruit off the pit as you can. Keep any odd slices or squashed bits for other uses, like a breakfast smoothie, or eat them as a cook's perk.

2 Halve the passion fruit and scoop out the flesh and seeds. Toss the mango slices with the juice of 2 limes, 1½ tsp superfine sugar, and most of the passion fruit flesh and seeds (keep some back for decoration). Cover and chill for about 10 minutes. If you leave it much longer, the lime softens the mango flesh too much.

3 Whip the cream with the lime zest, adding the rest of the lime juice and the rum at intervals. Don't overbeat. The cream should fall in soft folds. Add superfine sugar to taste.

4 Put the fruit into four glasses and spoon the syllabub on top. Finish with a drop of passion fruit on top of the cream.

and also...

mangoes with ginger, mint, and lemon grass
Put ½ cup water, ⅔ cup superfine sugar, a 1-inch cube fresh ginger (peeled and sliced), 1 lemon grass stalk (bruised and chopped), and the juice of 2 limes into a saucepan and slowly bring to a boil. Cook for 7 minutes and add a handful of mint leaves. Let the syrup infuse as it cools, then strain it and chill. Prepare 2 mangoes as above, cutting off the cheeks. You are only going to use the cheeks for this, so save the rest of the flesh for something else. Lay the cheeks on a cutting board and cut each one in slices, holding on to the mango flesh so that it stays together in the cheek shape. Carefully place each sliced cheek in a broad, shallow bowl and pour the syrup over the slices. Add a handful of small mint leaves and serve cold.

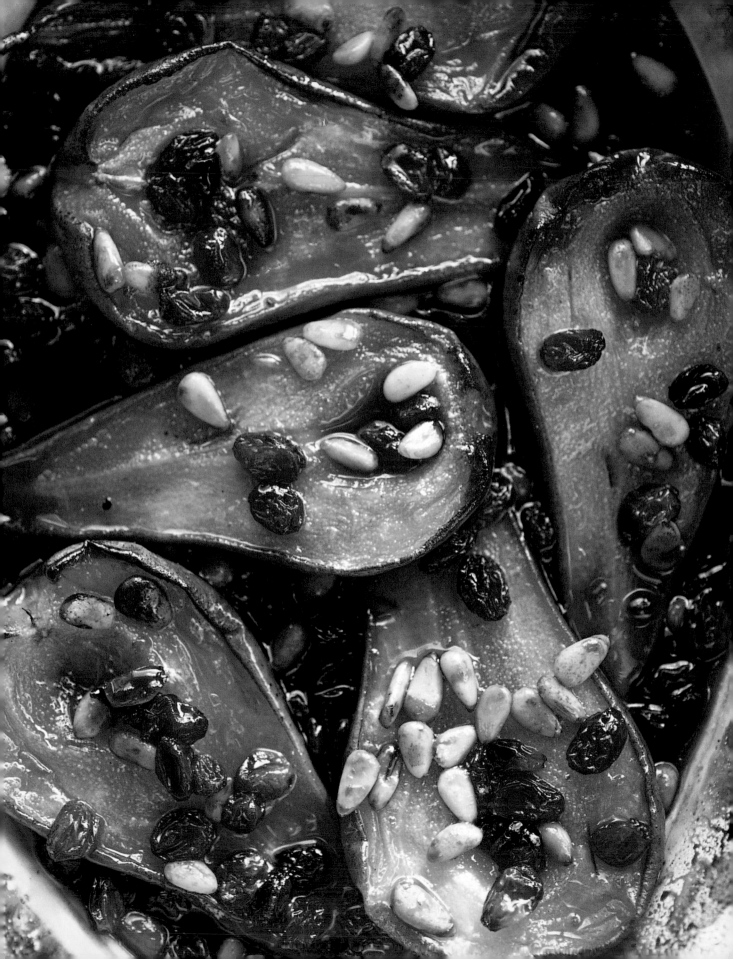

This makes a lovely, rustic-looking, dark, and glossy dish. If you can't find Moscatel — an inexpensive Spanish dessert wine — use Moscato, Marsala, or medium sherry instead. Coarsely chopped hazelnuts or almonds will do just as well as pine nuts.

· · · · · ·

pears, raisins, and pine nuts baked in moscatel

serves 6

½ cup raisins

1⅛ cups Moscatel

6 slightly under-ripe pears, halved and cored

¼ cup water

juice of 1 lemon

3 tbsp light or dark brown sugar

2 tbsp pine nuts

crème fraîche or Greek-style yogurt, to serve

1 Put the raisins in a small saucepan and pour on the Moscatel. Bring to a simmer, then remove from the heat and leave the raisins to plump up for about 30 minutes.

2 Preheat the oven to 350°F. Lay the pears, cut-side up, in a single layer in a shallow ovenproof dish. Spoon the raisins around them — if they're put on top, they will burn. Pour on the Moscatel, water, and lemon juice. Sprinkle the brown sugar on top of the pears and around them. Bake for 45 minutes, or until the pears are tender and starting to wrinkle at the edges. From time to time, spoon the juices over the top. Add the pine nuts midway through cooking.

3 Serve at room temperature, with crème fraîche.

and also...

baked pears stuffed with chocolate and hazelnuts
Halve and core 6 pears. Crush 3 vanilla wafer cookies, ¾ cup hazelnuts, and 2 tbsp light brown sugar together. Add a small beaten egg and 3 oz chopped dark chocolate. Spoon the filling into the core cavities and over the pears, sprinkle with 3 tbsp light brown sugar and bits of butter (use about 1 tbsp). Bake as above, with 1 cup sweet wine, ¼ cup water, and the juice of 1 lemon poured around the pears. Sprinkle on coarsely chopped toasted hazelnuts.

You could use walnuts or hazelnuts instead of pecans here. Good for both dessert and afternoon tea.

• • • • • •

pear and pecan cake

As well as using seasonal fruit for crumbles and cakes, add variety by mixing in dried stuff: apricots, plums, and sour cherries. And don't forget fresh cranberries.

serves 8

4 pears, peeled and cored

9 tbsp salted butter, softened and diced

½ cup sugar, plus 1 extra tbsp

3 eggs, lightly beaten

finely grated zest of 1 lemon

¾ cup self-rising flour, sifted

1 cup toasted pecans, ground, keeping back some of the coarser bits in the mixture for decoration

2 tbsp whole milk

I Preheat the oven to 350°F. Cut the cored pears lengthwise into about ¼-inch-thick slices. Butter an 8-inch springform pan and line the bottom with parchment paper.

2 Put the butter, ½ cup sugar, eggs, lemon zest, flour, nuts, and milk into a food processor and process until smooth. Spoon the batter into the pan and arrange the pear slices any way you like on top. Make sure you pack them together well. Sprinkle with 1 tbsp sugar. Bake for 40 minutes. A skewer inserted into the center of the cake should come out clean.

3 Let the cake cool in its pan for 15 minutes, then remove it, peeling off the parchment paper on the bottom, and put it on a wire rack to cool completely.

1½ lbs baking apples, peeled, cored, and chopped

5 tbsp water

½ cup firmly packed light brown sugar

½ knob preserved ginger in syrup, finely chopped, plus 1 tbsp ginger syrup from the jar

22 ginger snaps, plus 2 extra cookies, crushed, for decoration

3 tbsp whiskey

½ cup shelled walnuts, coarsely chopped, plus a few extra for decoration

2 cups heavy cream

6 tbsp Greek-style yogurt

6 tbsp confectioners' sugar

I Put the apples and water in a pan with the brown sugar and chopped ginger. Bring to a boil, stirring a little to help the sugar dissolve. Simmer for 15 to 20 minutes, until the apples have completely collapsed and the mixture is quite thick. If your mixture is too runny, keep simmering and it will thicken as it reduces. Add the ginger syrup and leave to cool completely.

2 Coarsely break up the ginger snaps. Sprinkle the whiskey on them and mix with the walnuts. Whip the cream, beating in the yogurt, and add the confectioners' sugar.

3 Layer the components in a large glass bowl or in small glasses, finishing with some cream. Cover and leave in the refrigerator for a couple of hours or until the following day. Just before serving, sprinkle on the reserved ginger snaps and walnuts.

An easy autumnal trifle. You don't even need any cake!

• • • • • •

apple and ginger trifle

serves 6

1¼ cups freshly squeezed orange juice

¾ cup water

1 cup sugar

3 sprigs rosemary

juice of ½ lemon

2 oranges

3 blood oranges

1 grapefruit

1 ruby grapefruit

sweetened crème fraîche or whipped cream, to serve

Don't think this is ordinary;
it's a stunning-looking dessert. The
colors of the fruits sparkle together —
just as the rosemary works beautifully
with the citrus-fruit flavors. Little
almond cookies are good on the side.

• • • • • •

citrus fruit and rosemary compote

I Heat the orange juice with the water, sugar, and 1 sprig of rosemary, stirring to help the sugar dissolve. Bring to a boil, then simmer for about 20 minutes until slightly syrupy, leaving about 1⅛ cups liquid. Add the lemon juice and other rosemary sprigs. Leave to cool.

2 Cut a slice from both the top and bottom of the fruits so that there is a flat base at each end. Remove the peel and pith by setting the fruits on one of their flat bases and cutting from top to bottom, following the curve of the fruit and working your way around it.

3 Now cut each fruit into thin slices. Pick out any seeds and throw them away. Put the fruit in a shallow bowl (plain white or glass is lovely), pour over the citrus syrup with the rosemary sprigs, and chill.

4 Serve with crème fraîche.

and also...

spiced orange and red wine compote

In a saucepan, heat 2¼ cups red wine, 1⅛ cups orange juice, 2 cups sugar, 3 star anise, 1 cinnamon stick, and 3 strips each of lemon and orange zest. Stir to help the sugar dissolve. Bring to a boil, simmer for 12 minutes, then cool completely. Add 2 tbsp Cointreau, if you want. Prepare 9 oranges as above. Remove the zest from the syrup, then pour it over the orange slices. Chill, and then serve.

serves 6

12 figs, not too ripe

1 oz dark chocolate, cut into little chunks

3 tbsp coarsely chopped walnuts

2 oz marzipan, cut into little chunks

1¼ cups red wine

7 tbsp sugar, plus 3 tbsp for sprinkling

1½ tbsp crème de cassis (black currant liqueur)

to serve

¾ cup Greek-style yogurt

¼ cup mascarpone cheese

confectioners' sugar

Although I'd usually serve three figs per person, this is such a rich filling you only need two. It's better to use slightly under-ripe figs; they can withstand the cooking without falling apart.

• • • • • •

marzipan and chocolate stuffed figs in red-wine syrup

1 Trim the tip off each fig. Cut a cross in the top but don't slice right through — you want to end up with a fig that just gently opens like a flower. Press the fig open and stuff each one with the chocolate, nuts, and marzipan until you've used everything up. Carefully push the figs back into shape, without squeezing out the stuffing. Place them in a small ovenproof dish where they'll all fit snugly.

2 Preheat the oven to 350°F. Put the wine and 4 tbsp sugar into a saucepan and heat gently, stirring a little to help the sugar dissolve. Turn the heat up and boil the liquid until it's reduced by a third. Add the cassis. Pour the syrup around the figs, spooning a little of it over each fruit, then sprinkle with the remaining 3 tbsp sugar (this will just help it to caramelize a little). Bake for 20 minutes. The figs should be soft, but not collapsing.

3 Mix the yogurt and mascarpone together. Add confectioners' sugar to taste (remember that you're serving it with something very sweet). Let the cooked figs cool a little and serve either warm or at room temperature with the cream.

A cheat's dessert, since it involves doctoring store-bought vanilla ice cream, but it's none the worse for that. Just make sure not to let the ice cream go as far as melting when you are trying to soften it — melted and refrozen ice cream can cause food poisoning. *Turrón* is Spanish nougat. If you can't find it, any nougat will do.

. . . . . .

figs baked in sherry with honey and turrón ice cream

serves 6

18 figs, not too ripe

1⅛ cups sweet sherry

5 tbsp light brown sugar

finely grated zest of 1 small orange

4½ oz soft turrón, or Italian nougat

3 cups good-quality vanilla ice cream

2 tbsp honey

I Preheat the oven to 375ºF. Halve the figs and pour ¾ cup of the sherry into a shallow gratin dish. Add 3 tbsp of the brown sugar and all of the orange zest. Set the figs, cut-side up, in the sherry. Drizzle ¼ cup of the sherry over the top and sprinkle on the remaining 2 tbsp sugar.

2 Roast for 15 to 20 minutes, until the figs are soft and the tops slightly caramelized. Let the figs cool.

3 Cut the turrón into little chunks. Slightly soften the vanilla ice cream and stir in the turrón and the honey, mixing well. Quickly get the ice cream back into the freezer to chill and firm up.

4 Pour the remaining 2 tbsp sherry over the figs once they're cooked (it just heightens the sherry flavor) and serve them, warm or at room temperature, with the ice cream.

Cold-weather desserts don't have to be tawny in color. Autumn brings scarlet cranberries, crimson pomegranates, and purple figs, and citrus fruits are at their best during winter.

Granitas may seem too cold for autumn and winter, but sometimes after a plate of filling comfort food it's exactly what you need. Frosted glasses filled with colorful shards of ice can look spectacular too.

It's now possible to find bottles of pure pomegranate juice quite easily. If blood oranges aren't in season, you can use a carton of squeezed juice.

· · · · · ·

pomegranate, blood orange, and campari granita

serves 6

1¼ cups pomegranate juice

1 cup freshly squeezed blood-orange juice

juice of 1 lemon

6 tbsp sugar

7 tbsp Campari

pomegranate seeds (optional)

1 Gently heat the fruit juices and sugar together, stirring a little to help the sugar dissolve. Leave to cool, then add the Campari. Pour into a shallow container and freeze, stirring the mixture with a fork about four times during the freezing process, which will take about 12 hours.

2 Spoon into glasses and sprinkle some pomegranate seeds on top.

and also...

cranberry and port granita

Put 12 oz fresh cranberries into a pan with 1¼ cups water. Bring to a boil and simmer for about 5 minutes, or until the fruit is soft. Push the fruit through a sieve and leave to cool. In another pan, heat 2½ cups superfine sugar and 2¼ cups water, stirring a little to help the sugar dissolve, then simmer for 5 minutes. Leave this to cool, then mix it with the fruit puree and 7 tbsp port. Continue as above.

apple and calvados granita

Put 2½ cups water and ¾ cup superfine sugar in a pan, and heat gently until the sugar has dissolved. Add 1 lb apples, peeled and chopped, and cook until soft. Cool and puree in a food processor with the juice of ½ lemon and 5 tbsp Calvados (or brandy). Continue as above. Serve in chilled glasses with more Calvados poured over each serving.

serves 6

1½ lbs baking apples, peeled, cored, and chopped

10 oz blackberries

¾ cup sugar

a slug of crème de cassis or crème de mûre
(black currant or blackberry liqueurs; optional)

9 tbsp all-purpose flour

9 tbsp whole-wheat flour

¾ cup cold salted butter, cut into cubes

⅔ cup firmly packed dark brown sugar

½ cup toasted bread crumbs

⅔ cup shelled hazelnuts

In autumn and winter I like crumbles to be nutty, with a flavor of burnt sugar like this one. You can use walnuts or pecans here too, or a mixture of nuts. I grew up in the countryside, where blackberry picking was just something you did, but it's harder to get your hands on them in the city. If you're making this outside blackberry season or simply can't find any, use blackberries canned in natural fruit juice instead. Just drain them.

· · · · · ·

I Preheat the oven to 350°F. Put the apples and blackberries into a pie dish and add the sugar. Mix to make sure all the fruit gets coated and drizzle on a little of the liqueur.

2 In a food processor, pulse together the flours, butter, and brown sugar until the mixture looks like bread crumbs. Add the bread crumbs. Chop the hazelnuts very coarsely — some should be left whole, in fact; you want a good chunky crumble — and add them to the flour mixture. Pat the crumble mixture on top of the fruit and bake for 35 to 40 minutes. The fruit should be completely tender and the top brown and bubbling.

hedgerow crumble

Flavored creams are wonderful for jazzing up simple cakes or fruit. The quantities of flavoring and sugar given are guidelines only. You need to adjust them, depending on what they're being served with. Add the flavorings as the cream starts to hold its shape. Adding anything acidic, such as lemon juice, will immediately thicken cream.

· · · · · ·

flavored creams

ginger and lime cream

Beat 1¼ cups heavy cream with 2 tbsp ginger marmalade and some finely chopped preserved ginger. When it begins to stiffen, beat in the juice and grated zest of 2 limes. It shouldn't need sweetening, but add light brown sugar if you like. Good with sliced mangoes or a mixture of melons.

brown sugar cream

Stir ¼ cup heavy cream into 1¾ cups Greek-style yogurt. Sprinkle with 7 tbsp dark brown sugar. You can either leave this to form a soft dark crust, or gently stir it in to marble the mixture. Great with stewed or baked apples and warm ginger cake.

maple cream

Beat 1¼ cups heavy cream and add 4 to 5 tbsp dark maple syrup. Squeeze in a good bit of lemon juice and stir. Taste to see if you want to adjust anything. Very good with apple and pear desserts.

cassis cream

Beat 1¼ cups heavy cream and stir in 2 tbsp confectioners' sugar and 5 tbsp crème de cassis (black currant liqueur). Good with plain red berries.

marmalade and orange-flower cream

Beat 1¼ cups heavy cream and, as it starts to thicken, add ¼ cup marmalade. Beat in 1 tbsp orange-flower water and add confectioners' sugar to taste. You can also add whiskey to this instead of the flower water. Great with chocolate or orange cake.

elderflower cream

Beat 1 cup Greek-style yogurt and 7 tbsp heavy cream together. Add ¼ cup confectioners' sugar and a good squeeze of lemon juice. Stir in ¼ cup elderflower cordial. Taste and adjust accordingly (elderflower cordials vary in strength). Good with poached gooseberry and rhubarb desserts.

passion fruit cream

Scoop the pulp and seeds out of 4 passion fruit. Sieve this and remove half the seeds. Add the rest back to the fruit pulp. Beat 1¼ cups heavy cream until it's just holding its shape, then add the passion fruit and 3 tbsp confectioners' sugar. This is surprisingly good with raspberries and strawberries.

lemon curd mascarpone

Beat ½ cup mascarpone cheese to loosen it. Stir in 6 tbsp fromage blanc or crème fraîche and 1 cup good-quality lemon curd. Good with a cake, such as the rhubarb one on page 183.

boozy cream

Beat 1¼ cups heavy cream and, as it starts to thicken, beat in ¼ cup Calvados, amaretto, bourbon, Marsala, kirsch, or whiskey, and ¼ cup confectioners', superfine, or light brown sugar. Pick your booze to suit the dessert or cake it's to go with.

flour, eggs, sugar, cream

......

I love cakes that can just be mixed with a wooden spoon and thrown in the oven. Try orange-blossom water here instead of rose water. An orange-scented version is good with peach or apricot compote.

· · · · · ·

rose-drenched yogurt cake with summer berries

serves 8

syrup

1¼ cups water

14 tbsp sugar

juice of 2 limes

1 tbsp rose water

1¾ cups self-rising flour, sifted

1 cup ground almonds

9 tbsp sugar

a good pinch of salt

1 tsp baking powder

2 large eggs, beaten

1 cup plain Greek-style yogurt

⅔ cup sunflower oil

finely grated zest of 1 lime

to serve

confectioners' sugar

summer berries (raspberries and blueberries are great)

crème fraîche or Greek-style yogurt

1 To make the syrup, put the water, sugar, and lime juice into a saucepan. Heat gently, stirring to help the sugar dissolve. Bring to a boil and simmer for 7 minutes. Leave to cool, then add the rose water.

2 Preheat the oven to 350°F. Butter an 8-inch springform pan. Combine the flour, almonds, sugar, salt, and baking powder in a bowl and make a well in the center. Add the eggs, yogurt, oil, and zest and mix with a wooden spoon. Pour into the pan and bake for 30 minutes. A skewer inserted into the middle of the cake should come out clean.

3 Cool the cake in the pan for 10 minutes, then turn out onto a plate. Pierce all over with a skewer and pour the syrup over the warm cake. Dust with confectioners' sugar just before serving (otherwise the sugar sinks into the syrupy top) and serve with berries and crème fraîche.

flour, eggs, sugar, cream

An easy-to-do chocolate cake that you can quickly whip up for friends or children's birthday parties. If you're making it for children, you might prefer to use milk chocolate instead of dark chocolate for the icing, in which case you can sweeten the glaze with superfine sugar or sifted confectioners' sugar rather than dark brown sugar.

• • • • • •

all-in-one chocolate cake

serves 8

1 cup self-rising flour, sifted

a pinch of salt

½ cup cocoa powder

3 large eggs, beaten

¾ cup sugar

¾ cup salted butter, slightly softened and diced

2 drops vanilla extract

¼ cup warm water

icing

6 oz good-quality dark chocolate, broken into small pieces

5 tbsp sour cream

5 tbsp heavy cream

5 tbsp dark brown sugar

decoration

toasted hazelnuts (a few whole, the rest halved or quartered) or toasted flaked almonds

confectioners' sugar (optional)

I Preheat the oven to 375ºF. Butter an 8-inch springform pan. Put all the ingredients for the cake, except the water, into a food processor or a bowl in which you can beat the ingredients with an electric mixer. Process or beat until combined. Add the water and mix again. Pour into the pan and bake for 25 to 30 minutes. The cake is ready when a skewer inserted into the middle comes out clean. Turn out and leave to cool.

2 To make the icing, put everything in a bowl set over a pan of simmering water and allow to melt. Stir everything together, take off the heat, and leave to cool and thicken. Spread this over the cake with a palette knife. Decorate with nuts and sift over a light dusting of confectioners' sugar.

A version of the near-miraculous and eternally popular Australian lemon pudding — miraculous because, as the pudding cooks, a luscious layer of sauce forms beneath the sponge. Couldn't be simpler.

• • • • • •

baked lime and passion fruit pudding cake

serves 6

¼ cup salted butter, softened and diced

1½ cups sugar

finely grated zest of 2 limes

3 large eggs, separated

5 tbsp self-rising flour

1½ cups milk

juice of 2 limes

3 ripe passion fruit

confectioners' sugar, to serve

whipped cream, to serve

I Preheat the oven to 350°F. Butter a 1-qt baking dish. Throw the butter, sugar, and zest into a food processor and process until light and fluffy. Add the egg yolks and blend. Add the flour, alternating with the milk. Blend until you have a smooth batter. Add the lime juice.

2 Halve the passion fruit and scoop out the pulp and seeds. Remove and discard about a third of the black seeds (you can sieve the pulp and add two-thirds of the seeds back into the pulp) and add the pulp and seeds to the batter. Pour the batter into a large bowl.

3 Beat the egg whites until stiff but not dry and, using a large metal spoon, fold into the batter. Spoon into the baking dish and set in a roasting pan. Pour boiling water into the roasting pan to come about halfway up the sides of the baking dish. Bake for 1 hour.

4 Allow to cool a little when it comes out of the oven. Sift some confectioners' sugar over the top and serve with whipped cream.

Torrijas are basically Spanish French toast, if that makes any sense. They treat *torrijas* with some respect in Spain; it's not just a way of getting rid of a stale old loaf. This is a particularly classy treatment and makes an easy dessert. (Or have *torrijas* for breakfast if you feel like being a pig.)

I can't remember where I first came across honey ambrosia, but you always see jars of honey and nuts for sale in Italy and Greece for ridiculous prices. This, since you're making it, is cheaper. It's also better. Use decent honey and make sure the nuts aren't old. You can use dried apricots, chopped, instead of raisins, or a mixture of the two. The recipe makes more ambrosia than you need for four people, but just keep the rest for the next time (or have it on Greek-style yogurt for breakfast).

• • • • • •

torrijas with honey ambrosia

serves 4

ambrosia

¼ cup raisins, preferably a really good variety such as muscat

5 tbsp medium-sweet sherry

3 oz hazelnuts and blanched almonds, toasted and very coarsely chopped (you want some good big chunks and halved nuts in the mixture)

¾ cup honey

torrijas

2 large eggs, plus 1 large egg yolk

6 tbsp heavy cream

2 tbsp sugar

2 tbsp sweet sherry

4 thick slices soft white bread or brioche

¼ cup unsalted butter

confectioners' sugar, for dusting

I To make the ambrosia, put the raisins and the sherry in a small saucepan. Heat gently, then remove from the heat and leave the raisins to plump up for 30 minutes to 24 hours.

2 Add the nuts and honey to the raisin and sherry mix in the saucepan and heat until bubbling. Simmer for 3 to 4 minutes. Pour into a gravy boat, if you're going to use it immediately, or into a sterilized jam jar to store it.

3 For the torrijas, beat the eggs and egg yolk with the cream, sugar, and sherry in a wide, shallow bowl. Cut each slice of bread in half and coat the pieces in the egg mix, then leave them for about 5 minutes to absorb the liquid. This will give you lighter torrijas.

4 Melt the butter in a large frying pan until foaming and cook the bread for about 3 minutes on each side until golden brown. Serve each person two pieces of bread, dusted with confectioners' sugar and drizzled with the ambrosia.

This is a good blueprint to use for other fruit-topped cakes. Instead of rhubarb you could try sliced peaches, nectarines, plums, pears, or apricots. You just need to make sure your fruit is tender and ripe — any hard, unripe fruit won't soften in the forty minutes it takes the batter to bake.

• • • • • •

rhubarb cake

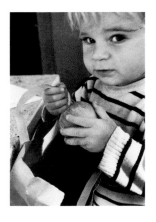

serves 8

9 tbsp salted butter, softened and diced

⅓ cup sugar, plus 5 tbsp for the rhubarb

3 large eggs, beaten

1 tsp vanilla extract

1 cup self-rising flour, sifted

2 to 3 tbsp milk

1½ lbs rhubarb, trimmed and cut into 1-inch lengths

confectioners' sugar, for dusting

I Preheat the oven to 375ºF. Butter an 8-inch springform pan. Beat the butter and sugar together until pale and fluffy. Add the eggs a little at a time, beating well after each addition. If the mixture starts to curdle, add a tbsp of the flour. Add the vanilla, then fold in the flour with a large metal spoon, adding enough of the milk to give the batter a reluctant dropping consistency. Scrape into the pan.

2 Toss the rhubarb with the 5 tbsp sugar and spread it over the top of the cake. Bake for 40 minutes. The rhubarb will be slightly singed in parts. The cake is ready when a skewer inserted into the middle comes out clean.

3 Leave the cake to cool in the pan, then carefully remove the ring and base. Dust with confectioners' sugar before serving.

Baking doesn't mean you have to don an apron and slave over a state-of-the-art food mixer. There are plenty of cakes for which you need nothing more than measuring cups and a wooden spoon or hand mixer.

flour, eggs, sugar, cream

I am very bad at baked rice pudding. Somehow I always manage to use either not enough milk or too much, so now I do this stove-top version. It's a snap, and quicker to make than the oven-baked version too.

· · · · · ·

chilled rice pudding with orange, honey, and cardamom syrup

and also...

with sour cherries in rose syrup

Put ¾ cup sugar and 1¼ cups dry white wine in a saucepan and heat gently, then bring to a boil, and simmer for 5 minutes. Add 1⅓ cups dried sour cherries. Let the fruit simmer for 2 to 3 minutes, then take the pan off the heat. Add the juice of 1 lime and 1½ tsp rose water. Allow to cool. You can serve the cherries at room temperature or chill them.

with pomegranate and blood-orange sauce

Squeeze the juice from 1 pomegranate (do it just as if it were an orange) and put it into a saucepan with ¾ cup blood-orange juice, 2 strips of orange zest, and 7 tbsp sugar. Gently bring to a boil, then simmer for 5 minutes. Leave the syrup to cool, remove the orange zest, and add the seeds of 2 pomegranates.

serves 4

¾ cup short-grain rice

4 cups whole milk

3 tbsp sugar

½ cup heavy cream

3 tbsp Greek-style yogurt

a couple of drops of vanilla extract

syrup

6 tbsp honey

3 tbsp water

juice of 2 oranges

crushed seeds from 4 cardamom pods

finely grated zest of 1 orange

I Put the rice in a saucepan and cover it with water. Boil for 4 minutes, then drain. Put the rice back in the pan with the milk and sugar and bring to a boil, then turn down to a simmer. Cook for 20 to 30 minutes, until all the liquid has been absorbed and the rice is soft. You need to stir from time to time and add a little more milk if you find it has been absorbed before the rice is soft.

2 Take the pan off the heat. Stir half the cream and yogurt and all the vanilla into the rice. Taste to check the sweetness, bearing in mind that the syrup is sweet. Leave to cool, then chill. When chilled, the pudding will be very firm, so before serving, loosen it by stirring in the rest of the cream and yogurt — and maybe even a little milk if needed.

3 Put everything for the syrup (except the zest) into a small saucepan and bring to a boil. Boil to reduce to a syrup (remember: it will thicken as it cools). Strain to remove the cardamom, then add the zest, and cook for another minute. Leave to cool. Serve with the rice pudding.

1½ cups dried apricots, coarsely chopped

⅔ cup golden raisins

1 cup Moscatel (a Spanish dessert wine)

1¼ cups whole milk

1¼ cups heavy cream

a pinch of salt

½ tsp vanilla extract

3 large eggs, plus 1 large egg yolk

½ cup sugar

3 tbsp salted butter

about ½ lb bread (soft white rolls or brioche are particularly good), sliced

confectioners' sugar, for dusting

crème fraîche or cream mixed with Greek-style yogurt, to serve

Bread pudding is one of the great glories of British cooking, and it requires no skill and very little effort to make. I turn out lots of different versions, so once you have the basic recipe in your head, play around with it. You can use Moscato or any other sweet dessert wine instead of Moscatel in this apricot version, or sherry, Madeira, or Marsala.

. . . . . .

apricot and moscatel bread pudding

1 Put the apricots, raisins, and Moscatel in a saucepan. Bring to a boil, then turn off the heat at once, and leave to soak for a couple of hours to overnight.

2 Bring the milk, cream, and salt to a boil in a heavy-bottomed pan. Add the vanilla. Beat the eggs, extra yolk, and sugar together. Stir in the warm milk and cream.

3 Butter the bread and layer it, buttered-side up, in an ovenproof dish, sprinkling on the fruit and wine as you go. Strain over the egg-and-cream mixture and leave to soak for 30 minutes to make the pudding lighter. Make sure there's no fruit sticking out of the custard to burn.

4 Preheat the oven to 350°F. Put the dish in a roasting pan and add enough boiling water to come halfway up the sides of the dish. Bake for 40 to 45 minutes, or until puffy and set with a golden top. Leave to cool slightly, dust with confectioners' sugar and serve with crème fraîche.

and also...

chocolate and pear bread pudding

Make the pudding as above, but layer the bread with 3 sliced, cooked pears (poached in 1 cup water, 6 tbsp sugar, and the juice of 1 lemon) and 4 oz dark chocolate, cut into chunks.

marmalade and whiskey bread pudding

Make as in the first recipe, but instead of the apricots and Moscatel, soak 2 cups raisins in 1 cup whiskey. Layer the bread with the soaked fruit and 10 tbsp marmalade spread on the buttered bread.

lemon curd and blueberry bread pudding

Make as in the first recipe, but layer the bread with 10 tbsp lemon curd, spread on the buttered bread as you go, and 1 cup blueberries.

If you don't have an ice-cream machine, making your own can be a bit of a slog (all that hand stirring during freezing), but there are some spectacular ice creams on the market just waiting to be personalized.

· · · · · ·

what to do with a tub of good ice cream

toppings for ice cream

passion fruit and orange sauce

Scoop the pulp and seeds out of 4 passion fruit and press through a sieve. Put ¾ cup orange juice in a saucepan and add the passion fruit juice plus 2 to 3 tbsp of the sieved seeds along with ¼ cup sugar. Bring gently to a boil, then simmer over medium heat for 12 minutes, until slightly syrupy. Take off the heat and leave the sauce to cool — as it cools, it will thicken.

apricot and elderflower sauce

Cover 2 cups dried apricots with 2½ cups water. Add the juice of 2 lemons and simmer very gently over low heat for 30 minutes, until the fruit has plumped up and is soft. Leave to cool, then puree with 5 tbsp elderflower cordial. Elderflower cordials come in different strengths depending on the brand, so taste to judge whether you want to add more or not.

hot fudge sauce

Put ¾ cup heavy cream, ½ cup dark corn syrup, ¾ cup brown sugar, and a pinch of salt into a saucepan and stir over low heat until the sugar dissolves, then add 1 oz chopped chocolate. Cook over low heat for about 15 minutes, stirring often, until it thickens. Add 2 tbsp butter and stir to melt. Brilliant with sautéed apple slices and vanilla or nut ice cream.

marmalade sauce

Put ½ cup marmalade into a small saucepan with ¼ cup dark corn syrup, ¼ cup orange juice, and the juice of 1 lemon. Bring gently to a boil, pressing the marmalade with a wooden spoon to break it down, and serve hot or warm. Divine with a mixture of vanilla and chocolate ice creams.

ginger, lime, and lemon grass syrup

Put ⅔ cup water; ⅔ cup sugar; a sugar-cube-sized knob of fresh ginger, peeled and chopped; the juice of 2 limes (save the zest); and 2 lemon grass stalks, bruised and chopped, into a saucepan and bring to a boil, stirring to help the sugar dissolve. Boil for 7 minutes, then leave the syrup to cool and infuse for a good 40 minutes. Strain, add the lime zest, and keep in the refrigerator. Good with vanilla or coconut ice cream, especially along with slices of fresh cold melon, pineapple, or mango.

christmas sauce

Put 7 oz good-quality mincemeat into a saucepan and add ¾ cup fresh cranberries and 2 tbsp orange or apple juice. Heat gently, then simmer for 10 minutes until the cranberries are soft but haven't burst. Add a slug of port or brandy and serve warm. Good with plain vanilla or a nut ice cream.

hot chocolate sauce

Melt 4 oz dark chocolate in a bowl set over a pan of simmering water. Add 7 tbsp dark corn syrup and stir until melted. Add 2 tbsp any spirit or liqueur (rum, brandy, crème de framboise, or Cointreau). Good with vanilla or coffee ice cream.

burnt sugar sauce

Put 1¾ cups sugar into a saucepan with 1 cup water and ¼ cup lemon juice. Bring to a boil, stirring to help the sugar dissolve, then let it boil to form a rich brown caramel. Take the pan off the heat and quickly add 1 cup heavy cream (stand well back as the caramel will spit). Stir and serve warm. Good with vanilla ice cream.

hot boozy cherries

Melt 2 tbsp unsalted butter in a frying pan and throw in about 1 lb pitted cherries. Add ½ cup sugar and the juice of ½ lemon. Keep sautéing the cherries and moving them around until they are tender and you have a thickish syrup around the cherries. Add a good slug of kirsch or grappa and spoon over ice cream.

raspberry crush

Puree 8 oz raspberries in a food processor with 2½ tbsp confectioners' sugar. Sieve to remove the seeds. Coarsely mash 4 oz raspberries with a fork and add to the sauce. Taste to see whether you want more sugar. Good with vanilla ice cream.

mix-ins for vanilla ice cream

- Chocolate-coated coffee beans
- A crushed-up candy bar
- A third of a jar of jam
- Crushed chocolate-chip cookies
- Finely chopped preserved ginger and ginger syrup
- Smashed meringues — even better with raspberries
- A bag of crushed malted milk balls
- Chopped-up panforte or nougat

desserts to make with vanilla ice cream

toasted brioche ice cream sandwich

Toast slices of brioche and while still hot, halve them and sandwich with grated dark or milk chocolate and softened vanilla ice cream. Dust confectioners' sugar over the top and serve wrapped in parchment paper.

fried panettone with melting ice cream

Fry slices of panettone in butter, sift confectioners' sugar over the top, and serve hot with warm sautéed apples or poached plums in winter, and sliced peaches or raspberries in summer, and good vanilla ice cream.

ice cream–stuffed baby brioche

Eaten in Sicily for breakfast but good after a lazy supper. Warm baby brioches in a low oven, then stuff with vanilla ice cream and raspberries. Top with toasted flaked almonds and a sifting of confectioners' sugar.

ice cream cookie layers

Sandwich your favorite ice creams with your favorite cookies. Put coffee or nut ice cream, for example, into chocolate wafer cookies.

berry vanilla cones

Buy cones and fill with vanilla ice cream, fresh raspberries, and raspberry crush (left).

a roll call of sundaes

- Poached pear, toasted hazelnuts, vanilla ice cream, and chocolate sauce
- Broken-up brownies, vanilla ice cream, raspberries, and raspberry sauce
- Fresh pineapple, coconut ice cream, a slug of Malibu, and ginger, lime, and lemon grass syrup (page 187)
- And there are always more . . .

Most of us eat carbs and starches at least once a day, so it's good to know how to make them properly; myths abound, especially about rice and couscous. Potatoes are covered in the vegetable chapters, so here's how to deal with the other starches we most commonly cook.

• • • • • •

an important bit about basics

couscous

A fabulous ingredient for the cook in a hurry. You can prepare couscous very quickly, and it can be as simple or elaborate as you like. All you need to do is put the couscous into a flat, shallow bowl and pour boiling water or stock over it. Allow two parts water to one part couscous. Stir in a couple of tbsp olive oil and season well. Cover the bowl with plastic wrap. Once the liquid has been absorbed (it takes 10 to 15 minutes), fork the grains to fluff them up and serve. You can do this in advance and leave the couscous to heat later, either by steaming, putting in a low oven (cover the dish with foil and heat at 350°F for 20 minutes), or microwaving it. Fork the couscous again to fluff it up after heating. You can also serve couscous at room temperature.

If you prefer a buttery finish to an oily one, then stir in melted butter once the water or stock has been absorbed. Only do this with couscous you want to serve hot, though, or the butter congeals.

Add fresh lemon juice or zest, shredded preserved lemon, and handfuls of chopped soft herbs (parsley, cilantro, and mint are all great). Embellish as much as you like, adding plumped-up dried fruit (sour cherries, cranberries, chopped apricots, figs, and raisins), sautéed onions (perhaps spiced with cumin, cinnamon, or red pepper), chopped fresh chiles, nuts (usually pine nuts, slivered almonds, or pistachios) and fresh fruit (pomegranate seeds, chopped apricots, or tomatoes).

bulgur wheat

Couldn't be easier or quicker, and bulgur has a gorgeous nutty taste. I now eat this more often than rice. Use two parts liquid to one part bulgur (you can use stock or water) and simmer gently, covered, for 10 to 15 minutes, until the liquid has been completely absorbed and the bulgur is fluffy. Leave the pan to sit, covered and off the heat, for 5 more minutes. Season and fluff with a fork.

As with rice, you can sauté some onion in butter or oil before adding the raw bulgur and liquid to the same pan. If you want to add other ingredients to make a pilaf, cook them separately and add once the bulgur is cooked. Olive oil, melted butter, herbs, and lemon juice are all good for improving the flavor. Beyond that, embellish it just as you would couscous or rice.

rice

I'm dealing here with long-grain rice, the type most often cooked as a side dish. White long-grain is subtle and fragrant; brown is nuttier and nutritionally better for you. Choose whichever seems right for the dish it is accompanying and allow about ½ cup per person.

To cook long-grain white rice, put the rice in a heavy-bottomed pan and add enough water to cover by

1 inch. Add salt, cover the pan, and bring to a boil. Cook vigorously for 4 to 5 minutes, turning the heat down if there is a build-up of steam in the pan.

Take the pan off the heat. If you take a peek under the lid (be quick so that the steam doesn't escape), you'll see that the rice looks "pitted," with lots of little holes in it. Leave the pan covered and allow it to sit for 10 minutes. The rice will cook in its own steam and absorb all the moisture. Check the rice to see whether it is cooked. If the liquid hasn't been completely absorbed, put the pan back on the heat for 2 minutes, then leave it to rest again for 5 minutes. If the liquid has been absorbed but the rice is still too firm, add a little water, put back on the heat for 2 minutes, then leave to stand for 5 minutes.

For long-grain brown rice, cook in a similar way to white rice but cover it with 2 inches water, cook vigorously for 8 minutes, then turn the heat down very low, leave covered, and cook for another 20 minutes on the heat, or until the water has been absorbed and the rice is soft and chewy.

You can cook both white and brown long-grain rice with stock instead of water, or sauté some chopped onion in the pan before adding the rice and stock.

It's okay to leave the cooked rice, covered, in a warm pan for 10 to 15 minutes before serving. Be sure to fluff the rice up with a fork before taking it to the table, and drizzle in some melted butter if you want.

You can add all sorts of herbs, onions cooked with spices, cooked vegetables, and dried fruits to dress the rice, and bits of warm cooked meat or fish to make a pilaf to serve as a main course.

pasta

Cook dried pasta in lots of boiling salted water. Salting the water improves the flavor, and an abundance of water gives the pasta room to move without sticking together. You don't need to add oil to the water, but you need to stir well once the water returns to a boil after the pasta has been added. This helps to separate the strands and lift pasta shapes from the bottom of the pan.

Allow 2 to 4 oz dried pasta per person. That sounds imprecise, but if you're serving pasta with a rich sauce (a creamy one, for example), you will serve a smaller portion than if you are dressing pasta with, say, a tomato sauce.

Drain pasta once it is al dente: this is just slightly firm to the bite. Overcooked pasta has a soggy texture and doesn't absorb sauce very well. You don't have to drain pasta too thoroughly, and you certainly don't need to pour water — either hot or cold — over it. Just put it into a heated bowl or back in the saucepan in which it was cooked and dress it immediately with the sauce. If you're in a tight spot and your sauce isn't ready yet, then douse the cooked pasta in olive oil or melted butter to keep it from sticking together and get the sauce together quickly.

Dried pasta is not inferior to fresh pasta; it is just different, and it is what most Italians eat every day. Much of the fresh pasta sold here has a mushy texture (though Italian specialty food stores often sell good stuff), so you're better off with the dried type anyway. With dried pasta, the more expensive Italian brands are usually of superior quality.

index

acknowledgments

This book has been created by an incomparable team. Commissioning editor Becca Spry, photographer Jonathan Lovekin, designer Miranda Harvey, editor Susan Fleming, and home economist Sarah Lewis have been a joy to work with, putting more time and effort into the project than their jobs — strictly speaking — require. I would particularly like to thank Jonathan, Miranda, and Sarah for making the shoot days so much fun. More often than not, it was like being on vacation. Jonathan just "got" a feel for what we were trying to achieve and then surpassed what we had in mind. We can't divine why his pictures are so brilliant because he just seems to turn up, chat, take a few snaps, and then enjoy lunch. But we're thrilled that they are. Sarah was always half a dozen steps ahead of me and is the most patient, kind, intuitive, and visual collaborator a cook could hope for in the kitchen. I can't thank them enough.

Thanks too to my sister, Lesley, my parents, Robin and Joan, and my friend Eleanor Logan for tasting and testing and generally hanging out in my kitchen. Eleanor surpassed what a friend reasonably can be expected to do by eating more cakes and desserts than is good for a girl. My lovely friend Jenny Abbott has been telling me for years that this book is the thing that would most improve her life (actually she's already had most of the recipes over the phone or scribbled on bits of paper), so I'm glad she kept nagging me about it. And I hope it will live up to her expectations. . . .

No work would get done without my lovely nannies, Mari Smit and Milante Lombard, who look after me as much as they do the children and manage to be friends/personal assistants/sisters and extra mothers all at the same time. My friends Aliza O'Keeffe (who thinks she can't cook but can) and Johanna Oldroyd (a great baker and my personal expert in all things Scandinavian) generously gave recipes for dishes they have cooked and I have loved.

Lastly thanks to my gorgeous boys, Ted and Gillies, who put up with their mom being stuck at the computer or the stove rather a lot of the time. Ted is only eight years old but took the beautiful photograph on page 38 (thank you for letting him, Jonathan), so he is obviously a food lover. Actually, this book would never have happened if Ted's arrival hadn't had such an impact on my life and my cooking. The fact that Gillies then came along and can enjoy that cooking is the — very considerable — icing on the cake.